Drop Of A Hat: Drama Lessons, Games

Drop of a Hat is for any teacher who wants to bring the curriculum to life through drama and creativity. Each lesson is based on a story, poem or theme and divided into bite-sized sections. If you're looking for a quick fix, just choose a couple of activities. If you're new to drama, there's a section at the back describing the games and strategies in detail.

You'll find approaches for using drama to raise standards in literacy and to explore stories, characters and themes. Topics covered include global warming, looking after pets, dealing with bullying and exploring issues around refugees. There are over a dozen activities for using drama in science as well as a lively introduction to Shakespeare's 'A Midsummer Night's Dream'.

These drama games and strategies are extremely adaptable and can be applied to so many subjects and themes. You'll discover a myriad of ideas you can pick up and use — at the *Drop of a Hat*.

David Farmer began exploring the power of drama as a learning medium while training and practising as a primary teacher. He set up TIE Break theatre in education company in Norwich, UK in 1981 and developed the use of drama and performance to explore stories, social issues and curricular topics through productions toured internationally.

In 2005 he began writing and publishing books, developing a website and courses on educational drama, as well as providing advice and support to schools and organisations worldwide. His experience with drama has led him to a belief in its power as a hugely effective learning technique and agent of change. This book brings together many of the approaches gathered and developed throughout his career in a format that will be of value to many teachers.

Other books by David Farmer

101 Drama Games and Activities

101 More Drama Games and Activities

Learning Through Drama in the Primary Years

Playful Plays (Volume One)

DROP OF A HAT

Drama Lessons, Games and Activities

David Farmer

Illustrated by John Shelley

dramaresource.com

© David Farmer 2021

Written by David Farmer

Cover Design and Layout by Anne Reekie

Illustrations by John Shelley

Thanks to...

All the creative students, teachers and student teachers from across the world who have attended workshops, courses and CPD (both live and online) with David Farmer, where these lessons were trialled and developed. Narayani Guibarra for her inspired and calm assistance at workshops over many years, NILE (Norwich Institute of Language Education), Victoria Walker-Pope and Annie Bartley at The International School of Amsterdam and all the enthusiastic children who took part in the workshops there.

Published by Drama Resource

www.dramaresource.com

ISBN 978-1-8383559-0-6

LESSON PLANS

INTRODUCTION

WHO THIS BOOK IS FOR

Drop of a Hat is aimed at any teacher who wants to bring the curriculum to life through creative drama teaching methods. It's designed so that you can simply flick through it, pick an idea and try it out.

The focus of the book is on using drama as a method of teaching and learning across the curriculum. You don't need to be a drama teacher to use it. In fact, the book is aimed at classroom teachers, teaching assistants and practitioners with any level of experience. If you want to read more about the drama games and strategies, a section at the back provides additional detail.

WHY DRAMA?

Dramatic play is already familiar to children as one of the main ways in which they learn before starting school. Imaginative thought, role play and make-believe are inherent skills which drama games and strategies tap into. Why *not* use drama when it enables children to internalise their understanding of subjects and topics through active and fun engagement with their peers?

Drama appeals to a wide range of children because it engages the senses and the emotions, deepening empathy and understanding. It helps to develop personal skills such as communication, cooperation, self-confidence and problem-solving.

Drama can be particularly effective for raising standards in literacy, including reading, writing, speaking and listening. It can be used to explore stories, characters and themes. Drama activities can act as a launch pad for work right across the curriculum.

DRAMA FOR LEARNING

Drama games and strategies can be used alongside other teaching approaches to make learning active and interactive. A wide range of educational drama techniques have been developed for use in the classroom and drama studio, based on groundbreaking work in past decades by practitioners such as Dorothy Heathcote, Gavin Bolton and Augusto Boal, to name just a few. Drama is a recognised method used widely by theatres, charities and agencies as an integral part of their education strategies.

Topics covered include global warming, caring for pets, dealing with bullying and exploring issues around refugees. There are over a dozen activities for using drama in science teaching as well as a lively introduction to 'A Midsummer Night's Dream'.

These methods and plans can be used to quickly initiate drama activity in the classroom but should not be viewed as rigid or prescriptive. Please adapt them to the ever-changing needs and perspectives of the students. We hope that they will spark further ideas for facilitating exciting ways to use drama across the curriculum.

GETTING STARTED

The book is divided into two sections: *Lesson Plans* and *Drama Games and Strategies*.

Each lesson plan is based on a story, poem or topic and divided into bite-sized sections. They can be used as complete ready-to-go sessions, or if you're looking for a quick fix, just choose a couple of activities and drop them into your own lesson plans in any order.

Each plan outlines:

- The target age group (key stage one is 5-7 years and key stage two covers 7-11 years). However these are not set in stone and most activities can be adapted for different age-groups
- A simple objective
- An estimated duration
- Resources that you may need

Most lesson plans consist of a double-page spread while others (*The Tiger Child p. 4* and *Funnybones p. 8*) include more than one session. Longer plans (*The King's Sentence p. 16, The Lost and Found Cat p. 30* and *A Midsummer Night's Dream p. 48*) span four or five pages. The section on *Science and Drama (pp. 36-47)* includes a range of ideas to enliven and support science teaching.

If you're newer to drama, or want a bit more explanation about an activity, the second part (*p. 53*) describes the drama games and strategies in more detail. After several of the lessons you'll find activity sheets and at the end of the book we have reproduced the beautiful illustrations by John Shelley for ease of photocopying.

DRAMA IN A CRISIS

ADAPTING DRAMA TEACHING FOR A NEW ERA

This book was written over a period of several years, before teaching practices were affected by COVID-19. In the long term we hope and anticipate that these activities will be enjoyed with full interaction in safe and healthy circumstances.

The drama lessons were originally designed to be used in halls, studios or classrooms. Where restrictions are in place, most activities can be adapted for enjoyable and productive online, socially-distanced or blended learning. This page outlines a few principles to bear in mind when adapting a session. Always ensure that you check the latest Health and Safety guidelines and your school procedures.

REMOTE (ONLINE) TEACHING

Online drama lessons are still subject to the same high expectations of student behaviour and responsibility. Maintaining your normal routines before and during lessons will help to ground your teaching and your relationship with the students.

Most drama activities can be undertaken using distance-learning platforms such as Zoom. The main meeting room can be used for whole class activities, while group work can be achieved using breakout rooms.

Physical Activities

For activities such as *Imaginarium* (pp. 58-59), students can respond individually to make physical shapes and movements. Where possible, encourage students to stand some distance away from the screen/camera so that they can use their whole body. Actions can be carried out on the spot instead of moving around the space.

Spoken Activities

For spoken pair or group activities, breakout rooms can be used if appropriate for the students. Short scenes or improvisations can be developed, rehearsed and then shared with the rest of the class back in the main meeting room.

If you are not using breakout rooms, an alternative is to simultaneously unmute two or more students in the main meeting room so that they can improvise together while the rest of the class practise audience skills by watching, listening and making constructive comments afterwards.

Using the chat function or mini-whiteboards are effective ways of enabling students to make written responses which would otherwise have been spoken, for example in discussions.

SOCIALLY-DISTANCED ACTIVITIES

Before beginning activities in a shared physical space, carry out a thorough risk assessment. Consideration needs to be given as to how students enter and leave a space as well as to how they work inside it.

Most drama activities can be adapted with social distancing in place. A common approach is to mark out a grid containing measured squares for each student so that they are kept aware of distancing throughout the session. Circle games can also work with social distancing. In good weather, outside spaces are a good choice for drama activities.

Guidelines vary, so we recommend that you take note of the most up-to-date regulations and recommendations at all times.

Further ideas, links and recommendations can be found at https://dramaresource.com/making-drama-out-of-a-crisis/

Scan the QR code to visit the above web-page:

THE MAGIC BOX

KS1/KS2 OBJECTIVE	DURATION	RESOURCES
Explore images in *The Magic Box* poem and lead on to the sharing of early memories	30 minutes	The poem *The Magic Box* uses evocative language to fire the imagination. It can be found in *The Magic Box* by Kit Wright. Wright, K. (2013). *The Magic Box*. Macmillan Children's Books. ISBN 978-1447250104

TIMING	CONTENT	RESOURCES
10 mins	**TEN SECOND OBJECTS** Divide the class into groups of four to six students. Each group is going to make the shape of an object, using everybody in the group, joining their bodies together in some way. The teacher calls out the name of an object then groups have just ten seconds to make the object. If this is the first time you are playing the game, begin with some easy objects such as a car, washing machine and helicopter. It's a good idea to demonstrate the game with one or two groups. After that all the groups can make each object at the same time. Use some of the objects listed below, which are linked to images in the poem and to the theme of the lesson. – Birthday cake, desert island, electric spark, fire-breathing Chinese dragon, (melting) snowman with a carrot nose, Tyrannosaurus Rex, magic box	*Ten Second Objects (p. 66)*
3 mins	**READ THE POEM** Sit in a circle. Explain that you are going to read a poem to the class, called *The Magic Box*. It is a poem which means something different to everyone who hears it. They should decide what it means to them and notice if any images come into their minds. Ask them to close their eyes. Read the poem aloud.	*Copy of 'The Magic Box' poem*
5 mins	**CIRCLE DISCUSSION** What did they think the poem was about? Take a few suggestions; there are no 'wrong' answers. What do they think is being put into the box? Ask for general ideas, such as memories, imagination, wishes and dreams, as well as specific images from the poem. You may find that between them, the class will remember most of the images including exact phrases. It's a very evocative poem.	
5 mins	**OUR MAGIC BOX** Discuss: If the children had a magic box, what memories would they put into it? Ask them to give examples of a happy memory, earliest memory, something that happened yesterday, a memory of home, a reminder of their family. Place an invisible (mimed) magic box in the centre of the circle. Invite children to share their memories. *What would you like to put into the box? Come forward to tell us your memory and sprinkle it into the box!* (Demonstrate a sprinkling action.) Allow a few minutes for individual children to step forward, speak their idea and 'sprinkle' it into the box.	

2 mins	**PARTNER SHARING**	
	Usually children will have lots of memories to share. If that is the case you can ask them to carry on the activity with a partner next to them.	
	Imagine you have a magic box between you. Take it in turns to sprinkle a memory into the box. How many can you come up with in one minute?	
	Remind them that they can use memories of family, school, home, favourite foods, holidays,	
5 mins	**PLENARY**	
	– Share the memories that children sprinkled into the box with their partner	
	– Can they use adjectives to describe their memories?	
	– What will the students remember most about this lesson?	
	– If there is time read the poem again	
	FURTHER DEVELOPMENT	*Freeze Frames (p. 56)*
	– Rehearse and perform the poem - bring verses to life with *Freeze Frames*	
	– Write a list of five magical things to put into the box linked to the five senses	
	– Write a list poem about a holiday, a place or early memories	
	– Make and decorate individual memory boxes, dream boxes or one for the whole class. Students can write ideas on slips of paper and post them inside	

THE TIGER CHILD 1

KS1 OBJECTIVE	DURATION	RESOURCES
Explore the story of 'The Tiger Child' through a range of fun and easy-to-do drama activities	35-40 minutes	Troughton, J. (1996). *The Tiger Child: A Folk Tale from India.* Puffin. ISBN 978-0140382389

Introduction

This lively folk tale from Orissa, India, explains why tigers eat their food raw and why cats live with people. The Tiger Child is sent to fetch some fire, but on the way he gets distracted by his friends. By the time he gets to the village, he has forgotten what he has been sent to fetch. He soon learns to appreciate the life the villagers have to offer.

The unit is divided into two parts, which can stand alone or in combination.

TIMING	CONTENT	RESOURCES
10 mins	**TEN SECOND OBJECTS** Divide the class into groups of four to six students. The members of each group have to work together to make the shape of an object with their bodies. The teacher calls out the name of an object then groups have just ten seconds to make the object. Before reading the story, ask the children to make the objects listed below. This will give added interest later, as all the objects are mentioned in the story. – Fire – Fish – Comb – Jungle	*Ten Second Objects (p. 66)*
5 mins	**SOUNDSCAPE** Show the children the cover of *The Tiger Child*. Ask them where they think the story takes place (jungle/rainforest). Explain that we are going to use sounds to create a picture of the rainforest. The teacher will act as the conductor, while students use their voices to 'paint' a sound picture of the jungle where the Tiger Child lives. – Invite suggestions for sounds which might be heard in the rainforest e.g. monkeys, insects, streams, birds, frogs, raindrops, creaking branches – If appropriate, allow everybody to choose their own sound – Control the shape of the piece by raising your hand to increase the volume or bringing it to touch your lap for silence – With a large class, divide the participants into sections, allocating a particular sound for each section, then conduct them accordingly	*'The Tiger Child' book* *Soundscapes (p. 61)*

8 mins	**TELL THE STORY** Read the story to the children. Show them the beautiful pictures which accompany the text. If you want to play *'What Happens Next?'*, make sure you stop at the point where the Tiger Child falls asleep in front of the fire.	
10 mins	**WHAT HAPPENS NEXT?** Explain that you have not reached the end of the story and that you would like the children to guess what happens next. – Divide the class into groups of 4-6 – Ask them to discuss what might happen next and to make a *Freeze Frame* showing their ideas (don't give them too long – just a few minutes) – Ask them to share what they've been working on – Use *Best Bits*, *Thought Tracking* or *Action Clip* to bring their ideas to life	*Freeze Frames* (p. 56) *Best Bits* (p. 54) *Thought Tracking* (p. 68) *Action Clip* (p. 54)
2 mins	**WRAPPING UP** – Finish reading the story – Were you surprised by the ending? – Did you enjoy using drama to learn about the story?	

THE TIGER CHILD 2

KS1 OBJECTIVE	DURATION	RESOURCES
Recap *'The Tiger Child'* story and explore the characters through a range of drama activities	30-40 minutes	Troughton, J. (1996). *The Tiger Child: A Folk Tale from India.* Puffin. ISBN 978-0140382389

TIMING	CONTENT	RESOURCES
10 mins	**STORYTELLING WHOOSH** Sit the children in a circle. Retell the story. When you mention a character or object, children step into the circle to act out that part of the story. Go round the circle in order so that children are allocated parts randomly. If more than one character is mentioned then a few players can step in together (e.g. villagers). If a character speaks, read out the words and ask the child playing the character to repeat the words. For repeated phrases (such as *'I have come for the thing my uncle wants...'*) invite the whole group to say them with you. When you finish a section of the story, clear the space by waving your hands dramatically and saying the magic word *'Whoosh!'* Everyone should go back to their places. After this, continue telling the story and pick the next child in the circle to play the next character.	*Storytelling Whoosh! (p. 64)*
10 mins	**TEACHER IN ROLE** The children will meet a character from the story who needs their help and advice. Explain that you will play the character (without revealing who it is — the Tiger). – The teacher leaves her chair and puts on a hat or scarf as a token costume. She sits down as the character and says *'I'm a bit sad and hungry because my fire has gone out and I can't cook my food.'* The children will soon realise which character is being portrayed – As the character, guide the children into a discussion about food they like: *'What food do you eat? Do you eat it raw? Really? Do you like raw food?'* Perhaps they can persuade the Tiger to try some new dishes – The Tiger can ask for advice about getting or making fire. *'How can I get fire from the villagers?'* This can lead on to ideas about creeping into the village in disguise; giving gifts to the villagers; trying not to frighten them by showing his sharp teeth; rubbing sticks together and so on – The teacher should draw out ideas and suggestions from the children about practical ways that they could help – The Tiger thanks the children for their advice and says goodbye – The teacher leaves and removes the token costume When the teacher sits down again as herself she can recap by asking the children what the Tiger said.	*Orange/yellow hat or scarf to denote the Tiger* *Teacher in Role (p. 65)*
	OPTIONAL The activity can lead to writing/drawing recipes for the Tiger or acting out ideas for getting fire from the villagers	

8 mins	**OFFERING OBJECTS**	*Orange scarf/hat*

Ask one child to sit in the centre of the circle to play the role of the Tiger Child. You can give them an orange scarf or hat to wear. Explain that the other children are villagers who are going to try to help the Tiger Child.

Can the children think of an object to pretend to bring to the Tiger Child? It can be an object from the story or something of their own choice. Nominate a child to mime bringing the first gift to the Tiger Child (for example, a fish or toy).

Use the following phrases from the story as dialogue (the children are likely to remember them) for the two characters to speak. The rest of the class can join in with the lines to support the players.

Tiger Child: *I have come for the thing my uncle wants but I can't remember what it is.*

Villager (offers a mimed object): *Is it a/an...* (bowl of milk, cushion, ball etc.)

The Tiger Child should play with/eat the mimed object before saying: *No I don't think it was that!*

Teaching Tip

If children are initially reticent the teacher should model how to respond as the Tiger Child.

8 mins	**PLAY IN PAIRS**	

After the group activity, children will enjoy repeating the game in pairs, with one offering objects and the other trying them out. Make sure they both have a turn at playing the Tiger Child! They may want to show/perform some of these.

	EXTENSION ACTIVITIES	*Freeze Frames (p. 56)*

- Write a recipe for the Tiger to make some delicious raw food dishes
- Draw a picture of the Tiger Child meeting different people in the village
- Draw a picture of your own pet and its favourite objects
- Link the story to a project on India
- Make up a story about another jungle animal with a problem, for example *The Elephant Who Lost Her Trunk*
- Play some relaxing Indian raga music while the children are working
- Show the book illustrations again and ask the children to make *Freeze Frames* of the images
- Make a 'Missing' poster for the Tiger Child

CREATE A SOUND JOURNEY

Make another soundscape like the one on page 4, but this time use it to create the sounds of the Tiger Child's journey from the jungle to the village.

Begin with quiet jungle sounds (insects, leaves, birds), then the sounds of the monkeys playing, the splashing in the pool, the sounds of the village and finally the sound of the cat, purring in front of the crackling fire.

FUNNYBONES 1

KS1 OBJECTIVE	DURATION	RESOURCES
An interactive storytelling session to explore the plot and characters of *Funnybones* through a range of drama and movement activities	45 minutes	Ahlberg, J. and A. (1980). *Funnybones*. Walker Books. ISBN 978-0140565812

TIMING	CONTENT	RESOURCES
3 mins	**BEGIN THE STORY** Introduce the story and tell the students they will do some drama activities to explore what happens. Explain that there are some parts which the children can join in with (e.g. the repeating text on the first page: *dark, dark...*) Read the opening of the book up to '*They went into the park*'	*'Funnybones' book*
10 mins	**SHOW ME** Divide the class into groups of 4-5. – Ask groups to make a *Ten Second Object* of the skeletons' house. They can also add spooky sounds! – Share some of the objects made by groups – Give groups another 60 seconds to make a *Freeze Frame* of what they think happens next in the park – Use *Thought Tracking* to find out what different characters in the freeze frame might be thinking or saying	*Ten Second Objects (p. 66)* *Freeze Frames (p. 56)* *Thought Tracking (p. 68)*
3 mins	**READING** Read up to where the skeletons put the dog back together and they sing a song to celebrate: '*These bones, these bones can bark again...*'	
10 mins	**MIXED-UP DOG DANCE** Divide the class into groups of 4-5 and explain that the children will make their own versions of 'mixed-up dogs'. They should make two freeze frames: – First, the dog bones scattered on the ground, with each student as a different bone – Second, the bones put back together in the wrong order After a couple of minutes choose one group to show what they've done in the centre of the space. Begin with the 'bones' disconnected on the ground, then play some atmospheric music. They should move in slow-motion into the second freeze frame, showing the shape of the mixed-up dog. Remind them to listen to the music and move *slow-ly*. Invite another group to do the same activity in the centre, making a new mixed-up dog each time. Once you have established the technique you can show two or three groups at the same time while the music plays.	*Music e.g.* *'Ghost Town' (The Specials)* *'Alladin Dub' (The Spy from Cairo)* *'Carnival of the Animals: Fossiles' (Saint-Saëns)* *'Nyakinyua Rise' (Jiin)*
3 mins	**READING** Read up to the page that ends '*and the dog skeleton frightened them.*'	

10 mins	**MIRROR GAME**	*Bell or Tambourine*

Explain that the skeletons are going to practise being scary by standing in front of a mirror. Demonstrate the *Mirror Game* with two students.

The pair should stand facing each other a short distance apart with an imaginary mirror in between. A is the skeleton and B is the reflection. A starts moving slowly, smoothly and scarily while B tries to reflect A's movements as accurately as possible. When they have got the hang of this, give a signal (clap your hands/play a bell) for the players to swap so that A is now the leader.

- Divide the class into pairs and ask them to label themselves A and B
- Play the game, emphasising slow movements
- Swap leadership a few times
- Give a theme such as morning exercises, getting dressed or singing a song
- Ask a pair to show what they were doing
- Give the signal to swap a few times then stop the activity and ask students to guess who is leading at that moment
- Repeat with more pairs

Teaching Tips
- Play some spooky music to help create the atmosphere
- When students swap over leadership they should make the change as smoothly as possible so that it is hard for others to guess who is leading!

Slow or spooky music e.g. 'Nocturne in E-flat Major, Op 9' (Chopin)

'Twice Variation' (Einaudi)

'Danse Macabre' (Saint Saëns)

1 min	**READING**

Read the story to the very end: *'They still do'*. The children can join in with *'dark, dark'* once again.

3 mins	**PLENARY**

- What was your favourite part of the story?
- What did you enjoy most about the drama lesson today?
- Is it easy to make freeze frames?
- Did you enjoy working with a partner in the mirror game?
- Did you know that there are lots more *Funnybones* stories?

FUNNYBONES   2

KS1 OBJECTIVE	DURATION	RESOURCES
Use a variety of drama games and strategies to further explore the story of *Funnybones*	35-40 minutes	Ahlberg, J. and A. (1980). *Funnybones*. Walker Books. ISBN 978-0140565812

TIMING	CONTENT	RESOURCES
10 mins	**SOUNDSCAPE** This activity can be done sitting on the floor or at desks. Remind the children of the story and ask them what they remember about the skeletons' house. What kind of sounds might they hear inside the house? Ask for suggestions, including names of sounds as well as vocal examples. These could include the staircase, creaking doors, the skeletons moving around, skeletons scaring each other, the dog barking, laughter, strange snoring... Explain that you are going to create a 'soundscape' or sound picture of the haunted house. As well as vocalising creepy sounds, ask the children to think of words from the story which they can speak in a spooky way (such as *'dark, dark'*. Divide the class into sections, giving a particular sound for each section. When everybody is ready, the teacher conducts the sounds by raising her hand to increase the volume or bringing it down for silence. Discuss how effective the soundscape was and how it could be improved. You may wish to record the result.	*Optional: Recording device* *Soundscapes (p. 61)*
10 mins	**A VISIT TO THE ZOO** In the story the skeletons meet the skeleton animals in the zoo. Show pictures from the book to remind the children of the animals. Divide them into groups of about five to make *Ten Second Objects* of some of the animals. Can any groups actually move around as the animal? If there is time, groups can make a different animal of their own choice for others to guess.	*Ten Second Objects (p. 66)*
	WHAT HAPPENED NEXT? Explain that the class are going to make up a new adventure for the skeletons, for example, what happened the next night, or what could happen if the skeletons went out during the day. Choose one of the following ways to extend and innovate the story: – **Imaginarium** can be done by the *whole class* in a circle – **Freeze frames** are made in *smaller groups* (Group work is generally more suitable for older students.)	
15 mins	**IMAGINARIUM (Whole Class)** The players sit or stand in a circle. One person steps forward and makes a freeze frame of an object or character that could appear in the new story. As well as making the shape, the player should announce what she is, for example, *'I am a lamppost'* or *'I am the skeleton dog'*.	*Imaginarium (p. 58)*

Imaginarium (continued)

Other players add themselves into the scene by making objects or characters related to ones that are already there. Everyone continues to hold their positions. The game ends when all players have stepped in or when enough ideas have been added. At this point the teacher says 'Whoosh!' and the players step back to the edge of the circle.

It is important that players watch and listen carefully so that they add in an appropriate character or object. Only one idea at a time should be added so that everyone can see and hear what is being included. Players should think about how their characters and objects relate to each other, how they can make interesting shapes and how they can use different levels (high, medium or low).

At the end you can ask students to improvise a short version of the story that has been created.

You can of course play the game more than once to try out ideas for different adventures.

Teaching Tips

- Two or more players can step in at the same time to make an object together
- The teacher can say *'Action!'* and everyone brings the scene alive for a few moments through improvised sounds and actions
- Use *Thought Tracking* to find out what characters/objects are thinking
- Ask players to add an adjective e.g. *'I am a shaky skeleton'*
- Ask players to speak a sentence describing what their character or object is doing

Action Clip (p. 54)

Thought Tracking (p. 68)

---

15 mins

FREEZE FRAMES (Groups)

This is an alternative way to devise new adventures. Divide the class into groups of 4-5. They should discuss and improvise their story before showing it to the rest of the class. They can use narration including key phrases such as *'On a dark, dark hill'.*

Freeze Frames (p. 56)

EXTENSION ACTIVITIES

- Draw a new adventure of the skeleton family
- Add speech balloons like the ones in the book
- Compose your own songs, raps and rhymes like the ones in the story
- Play warm up games like Grandmother's Footsteps and Keeper of the Keys to explore dramatic tension

---

SCARDY CATS

Discuss the different ways that the skeletons tried to frighten each other in the story.

In threes, children take the roles of the two skeletons and the dog and have to act out different ways of scaring one other. Can they act as though they are not expecting anything before they are surprised? Which group can make up the funniest idea?

CARING FOR PETS

KS1/2 OBJECTIVE
Learn that pets need to be looked after and should be treated with respect

DURATION
40-55 minutes

RESOURCES
Related education resources can be found on the RSPCA website, including 'The Five Animal Freedoms'

TIMING	CONTENT	RESOURCES
5 mins	**CLAP ACROSS THE CIRCLE (1)** Play this warm-up game to introduce the theme and encourage communication. You'll know if the game is working when it seems like an invisible ball of energy and sound is being passed around the circle. To begin, the group stands or sits in a circle. *I'm going to look at someone across the circle and clap towards them. So, Josie, I'm going to move my hands and clap towards you like this. Imagine the sound travelling towards you. Reach out and catch the sound with both hands as you make another clapping sound. Here we go!* *Now, Josie, can you choose somebody else and pass the sound on to them by clapping towards them? Perfect. Keep it going around the circle and make sure everybody has a turn.* **Teaching Tips** Remind students: – Clap to catch and clap to pass – Make sure you look at the person you are clapping to. If you don't make eye-contact, they won't know who you're passing to – If you have a large class you can divide them into two groups once you have demonstrated the game.	
5 mins	**CLAP ACROSS THE CIRCLE (2)** Play the game again, but this time introduce a category, for example *colours*. Each player should name a colour when they clap their hands towards the next person. If they can't think of a different colour they can repeat a previous one. The next category is *pets*. Each student should name a type of pet when they clap their hands. If they can't think of a different animal, they can say the name of a pet, e.g. Smudge, Tigger or Thumper. **Teaching Tip** – Encourage students to think of more than one pet while they are waiting for their turn in case someone else chooses the one they were thinking of	
5 mins	**DISCUSSION** Sit down and discuss – How many students have a pet? – How do they look after them? – Why do people keep pets?	

12

10 mins	**IMAGINARIUM**	*Imaginarium (p. 58)*

Sit in a circle. Explain that we are going to think about things that animals need to be happy and healthy. Choose one child to represent a pet (for example, a cat) in the centre of the circle. Now ask everyone to think of something that will help the cat to be happy. Go round the circle and ask each child to step in and make the shape of the object they have thought of, for example, bowl of water, toys, scratching post, bed, litter tray. Encourage them to also think of things to keep the cat healthy and safe, for example, vet, tablets, medicine, brush, microchip, flea collar.

When you have gathered enough ideas, say 'Whoosh!' and wave your hands to clear the space. Choose another child to be a different type of pet and repeat the game. Discuss which things were the same as the first pet and which things were different.

RSPCA website: 'The Five Animal Freedoms'

10-15 mins	**GUESS THE PET (MIRROR GAME)**	*Bell or Tambourine*

Select two students to demonstrate the *Mirror Game* and label them A and B.
- The pair should stand facing each other a short distance apart with an imaginary mirror between them
- A starts moving slowly and smoothly, while B tries to reflect A's movements as accurately as possible
- When they have got the hang of this, give a signal (ring a bell or clap your hands) for the leading to swap so that A is now looking in the mirror
- Now start again and ask A to think of a type of pet. They should slowly make the movements and facial expressions of the animal
- B copies the movements and afterwards guesses what the animal was

Now all the students are going to take it in turns to be different types of pet.
- Divide the class into pairs and ask them to label themselves A and B
- 'A' will be the first animal. Emphasise slow movements
- After a while ask them to stop and guess the animal
- Swap over. Partners pretend to be a different animal each time they swap
- Ask a pair to show what they were doing (they should whisper to decide who is leading at first)
- Give the signal to swap a few times then stop the activity and ask the students to guess who is leading at that moment and which animals they saw
- Ask more pairs to show their ideas

10-15 mins	**MIME EXERCISE**

- On your own, imagine you are looking after a pet
- Act out (mime) feeding, grooming and playing with the pet
- Introduce your imaginary pet to a partner
- How realistic can you make it?

EXTENSION ACTIVITIES
- In class, discuss different ways in which we can care for pets
- Draw a pet and around it draw five objects which are important for looking after pets

IF PETS COULD SPEAK

KS1/2 OBJECTIVE	DURATION	RESOURCES
A range of drama activities to explore understanding of pets and attitudes toward them.	45-55 minutes	Helpful education resources can be found on the RSPCA website

TIMING	CONTENT	RESOURCES
10 mins	**FREEZE FRAMES** Stand in a circle and turn to the person next to you. *Label yourselves A and B. A is a pet owner and B is a pet. You can decide what kind of pet in a moment. Make a freeze frame of an activity that the owner and pet are doing together, for example, feeding the pet, exercising it, looking after it. Now you have twenty seconds to decide what the pet is and to make the freeze frame.* *Sit down and let's look at some freeze frames. Who's got one that's ready?* Ask the class to guess what's going on in each freeze frame and what kind of animal the pet may be. If appropriate, use *Action Clip* to help students guess the pet and what the pair are doing. As you look at more pairs, discuss whether we always know what pets are thinking. As a lead-in to the next activity, you can use *Thought Tracking* to discover thoughts of the owner and the pet.	*Freeze Frames (p. 56)* *Action Clip (p. 54)* *Thought Tracking (p. 68)*
10 mins	**HOT SEATING** **Discussion** – *How do pets tell their owners what they need?* – *Do pets always enjoy their lives? Do they sometimes want to do things they're not allowed to? If you could talk to a pet, what questions would you ask it?* These questions can be written up for display. **Pair Activity** With your partner, swap over so the other person is a pet. Now try some hot-seating: the owner asks the pet questions and the pet answers in role. After a few minutes, swap over so that both partners get a chance to be in role. Some of these conversations can be shared. Example questions: *How old are you?* *Where do you sleep?* *What do you dream about?* *What's your favourite food?* *Can you read?* *What are your hobbies?* *What kind of music do you like?* *What's your earliest memory?* *What do you like best about being a pet?* *Are you ever unhappy?* *What's the funniest thing that ever happened to you?* *Are there some things you wish your owner would let you do?*	*Hot Seating (p. 56)*

| 10-15 minutes | ## WHERE DO YOU STAND? | *Thumbs up/ Thumbs down signs (pp.70-71)* |

This activity is a great way of encouraging discussion. Set up two signs, one saying *'Agree'* and the other *'Disagree'* or 'Thumbs up/Thumbs down' signs. Read out one of the following statements (or choose your own). Ask everyone to show what they think about the statement by standing between or near to one of the signs. Close to *'Agree'* means that you really agree - halfway between means that you're not sure. When everyone has moved into position, you can discuss their reasons for deciding where to stand.

Where Do You Stand? (p. 69)

Statements
- Pets make humans happy
- A big dog can look after itself
- Cats are perfect companions
- A tortoise can be 'man's best friend'
- Snakes are ideal pets
- It's cruel to keep pets in a flat
- Owners who don't clean up their animals' poo should be fined
- Birds are happy living in cages
- It's okay to keep a dangerous animal as a pet
- Animals have the same rights as humans

| 15 mins | ## SHOULD I GET A PET? | *Conscience Alley (p. 55)* |

This activity uses *Conscience Alley* to explore whether different types of people should get a pet. The class forms two lines facing each other, with a gap between them.

One student is given the role of a character and slowly walks down the alley. On one side, the students give reasons why the character should get a pet. They can also suggest what kind of pet the character should get.

On the other side, students try to persuade the character that it would be wrong to keep a pet. It is likely that some reasons will be repeated, but students should try to express themselves in their own words. When the student in role reaches the end of the alley, they should decide whether the character would get a pet.

Suggested characters
- A delivery driver who is away from home most of the day
- An older person living on their own
- A parent with two young children
- A strict headteacher
- The Prime Minister
- A famous pop star
- A footballer

EXTENSION ACTIVITIES
- Discuss whether the drama activities have helped the students understand more about pets
- Talk about the most important elements of caring for pets
- Compare the basic needs of humans and pets (the RSPCA provide teaching resources covering this)
- Make a grid or bar graph to show types of pets owned by the class
- Write, draw or act out a guide to looking after a pet

THE KING'S SENTENCE

KS1/2 OBJECTIVE
Explore the value of words and the power of non-verbal communication through a specially-written fable

DURATION
60 minutes, can be spread over more than one session

RESOURCES
Pencils and a box or hat containing small scraps of paper.

Examples of Deaf sign language (many short videos can be found with an online search)

Story Summary

'The King's Sentence' (begins on opposite page) is about a greedy King and Alexia, a girl who loves words. Unfortunately she talks too much in front of the King and he decrees that all words will be banned. The story describes how Alexia persuades the King to change his mind with the help of her imagination — and the wind.

- The lesson includes some phrase cards which can be found on pages 20-21

TIMING	CONTENT	RESOURCES
1 min	**INTRODUCTION** Explain that you are going to tell a story and the children are going to do some drama and discussion activities to explore and guess what happens.	
5 mins	**STORY PART ONE** Tell the class **Part One** of the story (opposite page).	
10 mins	**NON-VERBAL COMMUNICATION (1)** **Discussion** – What would it be like if words were banned? – Would people in the story be able to communicate without speaking? – Can the children think of how we use gestures to say yes or no? – Mention that gestures vary from place to place, so that nodding or shaking your head can have opposite meanings in different countries – Can students think of other gestures we use to communicate? – Demonstrate any of the following gestures and ask students what they mean – *Shrug, Wave, Folded arms, Pointing, Prayer hands, Thumbs up/down, Stop (like a traffic policeman), Winking* – Can the students think of gestures for the following? – *Okay, Sssssh! Come here, Peace, Love, Help!* If the students don't mention it, you can also talk about Deaf sign language. Ask for any examples that they know (see breakout box on opposite page).	

THE KING'S SENTENCE by David Farmer

PART ONE

There was once a king who wanted to rule everyone and everything.

Each year the people of the kingdom queued up to give the king half their money. Half their vegetables, half their fruit, half of everything. So the king got richer and richer and the people got poorer and poorer. But the richer the king got, the sadder he became and the more he wanted. He didn't just want to rule the people. He wanted to rule the animals. He wanted to rule the trees and the leaves. He wanted to rule the flowers, the rivers, the ants, the earthworms, the icicles, the bicycles, the bees, the seas and the fleas.

In the middle of the kingdom, in the middle of the ocean there was an island and on it was a thick forest. In the middle of the forest there was a small village and in the small village were some goats, sheep and cows. In one of the smaller houses lived a little girl called Alexia.

One day Alexia went with her family to give the king half the sheep and half the cattle and half of all their money. The family queued up outside the palace all day long.

Alexia was bored. 'Why is this taking so long?' she asked.

'Be quiet', shushed her mother, 'The king might hear you!'

But Alexia couldn't be quiet. Alexia was one of those girls who loves to talk. She loved saying words, hearing words and even singing words.

Before they knew it, the family were standing in front of the king. The palace was full of animals. There were sheep, cattle, hens, dogs, cats, rats, mice and lice. They were baaing, mooing, clucking, barking, miaowing, squawking and squeaking.

'Why does the king need all these animals? Where will he put them all?' asked Alexia.

Well, the king overheard what Alexia said and he looked furious. His face turned red, his eyes began to bulge, sweat appeared on his forehead, his nostrils opened wide and he started to huff and puff quickly like a steam engine. He opened his mouth so wide that everybody could see inside it. They could see his teeth and his tongue and his tonsils.

'How dare you!' roared the king. 'How dare you speak in front of the king!'

The king stood up and passed sentence on the whole country.

'No more words will be spoken. No more words will be sung. All words will be banned.'

DEAF SIGN LANGUAGE

Some people use non-verbal communication all the time, for example by using Deaf sign language. Ask the children for examples of signs that they know.

Hundreds of different sign languages are in use across the world. Here are some words (related to the story) you can look up online to share with the children in your local sign language:

Please/Thank you, King, Mountain, Sky, Girl, Boy, Clapping

THE KING'S SENTENCE STORY AND LESSON CONTINUES...

17

TIMING	CONTENT	RESOURCES
10 mins	**NON-VERBAL COMMUNICATION (2)** Ask a pair of students to stand up. Explain that you would like them to take it in turns to communicate to their partner without using words. In turn, give each of them a phrase to communicate such as: *I'm hungry; I'm sad; I'm tired; I don't know.* Divide the whole class into pairs. Ask them to take turns in communicating one of the phrases from the cards on the following pages - without using words. They may exchange cards with another pair when they have finished. Ask pairs to share what they've been doing and see if the others can guess their meaning.	*Phrase Cards (pp. 20-21)*
15 mins	**SHOPPING ROLE PLAY** **Discussion** Thinking about the story, what would life be like if words were banned? Are there some things that you would no longer be able to do? Imagine what it would be like trying to buy things in a shop without speaking. **Shopkeeper (Teacher in Role)** Pretend to be a shopkeeper. Ask one of the students to role play a customer and buy different items from you. Start with easy items, such as a banana or a book. You can have fun (and encourage the students' miming skills) by deliberately misunderstanding their initial attempts. For example, you can give the customer a monkey instead of a banana. The shopkeeper must also use mime to communicate. Now, ask another customer to buy something more complicated, such as a computer. **Pair Improvisation** Ask the children to get into pairs again and to label themselves A and B. Explain that A is a customer and must think of different things to buy from the shopkeeper (B). After a while they can swap round. Afterwards they will probably want to share some of their improvisations. It can take time to watch everybody, so try using 'Best Bits'.	*Teacher in Role (p. 65)* *Role Play (p. 60)* *Improvisation (p. 60)* *Best Bits (p. 54)*
10 mins	**FINISH THE STORY** Tell the class part two of the story (opposite page) and follow the instructions within the text.	
5 mins	**FINAL ACTIVITY** Give out some slips of paper. These can be kept in a hat or box. Ask each student to write down the word they caught and to put the paper back in the box. Now you can read all the words out! Further activities can include writing a story or poem using the words or collecting favourite words in a box in the classroom over a period of time. This can become a treasure chest of words to use in creative writing when stuck.	*Hat or box* *Pens/Pencils* *Slips of paper*

THE KING'S SENTENCE by David Farmer

PART TWO

The families went back to their villages. They worked hard every day on their farms to grow more fruit and vegetables for the king. Everybody was silent because all words had been banned. No one was allowed to say *atom*, or *beverage*, or *knees-up*, or *belly button*. Alexia found this very difficult because she loved words of every kind. 'What will happen to the words?' thought Alexia, 'if nobody speaks them and nobody sings them?'

And then Alexia had an idea. Some people say it was a brave idea. Some people think it was a mad idea. But it was Alexia's idea and she decided to do it.

(Ask the children for some suggestions; what do they think it was?)

Alexia started to write words down and she hid the words anywhere she could. When nobody was looking she would write down a word and hide it behind a leaf, in a squirrel's nest, under a stone – in any secret place she could find. But when she came back to look for the words they were gone. The leaf had blown away. The squirrel had shredded up the words with its teeth to thicken its nest and the stone had rolled into the river.

Alexia had another idea. This time when she wrote down the words she put them in a box. It was a strongbox her grandfather had given her with a lock and key. Alexia kept the key with her wherever she went. Every day she wrote down a new word and put it in the box. Nobody else knew what she was doing. The weeks went by, the months went by, the years went by. Soon the strongbox was full of words and there were no more words to write down.

Still the people took half the animals and half the money to the king every year. Nobody could complain because no one was allowed to speak. No one could cheer themselves up with a song because no one was allowed to sing. And every year the king made everyone line up: the trees and the leaves, the flowers, the rivers, the ants, the earthworms, the icicles, the bicycles, the bees, the seas and the fleas. They all bowed down before the king.

The only person who was allowed to speak was the king himself. And it wasn't much fun for him because no one was allowed to answer him. After a while even the king stopped talking and eventually all the words were forgotten. People became sad because they couldn't talk to each other. They couldn't tell each other how beautiful the world was. They couldn't sing songs or tell stories and the world was a sadder place. And saddest of everyone was the king himself.

One day, when Alexia was a teenager, she climbed up to the top of the biggest mountain in the whole country. On her back she carried the big box of words and in her pocket she carried the key. When she got to the top of the mountain she unlocked the box and the wind blew around her ears. The wind jumped into the box, lifted up the words and blew them all around the world.

People looked up into the sky and saw the white clouds of words come fluttering down. The words blew over the forests, across the seas and into the villages. They blew into the bakery, the post office and the goat farm. They blew into the windows of the palace, they waltzed across the ballroom, whirled up the stairs and into the royal bathroom where His Royal Highness was having a scrub. One of the scraps of paper landed gently inside the hairy nostril of the king.

The king's nostril twitched. The king blinked. The king sneezed. The king sneezed a giant sneeze. The word flew out of his nostrils and landed on his knees. The king (whose name was Kevin) picked up the word and read it to himself. His eyes lit up. The wrinkled corners of his old mouth began to lift. The king smiled and then King Kev laughed.

He quickly got dressed and summoned the Royal Court. 'I pass sentence.' he announced. 'I pass sentence on the world. There will be words. People will say words. People will sing words.' When the people heard the king's sentence they looked at each other. Then they looked up at the sky. Each person held out their hand.

(Ask the children: Can you hold out your hand? Imagine the cloud of words above you. Catch one of the words and make sure you don't let it go.)

Into each and every hand a word tumbled from the sky. Each person read the word and each person listened to the other words.

(Which word did you catch? Can you whisper your word to somebody else?)

From that day on people talked and people remembered the old songs. People told each other how beautiful the world was and people told each other stories. In the Palace a miracle took place. The king was happy because his guards spoke to him. They told him stories and sung him songs. From that day on, King Kevin never asked the people to bring their animals and fruit and vegetables to the palace again. And Alexia sat on top of the mountain writing poems and reading books until she was a very old lady indeed.

PHRASE CARDS for The King's Sentence (p. 18)

Photocopiable © Drama Resource 2021

Pleased to meet you!

Let's play a game!

I'm hungry

I haven't got any money

Good luck!

Come here please!

I'm angry

Be quiet!

PHRASE CARDS for The King's Sentence (p.18)   Photocopiable © Drama Resource 2021

I scored a goal!

Shall we go for a swim?

Have you seen my phone?

Where is the hospital?

I think it's going to rain

I've lost my dog

Would you take my photo?

I'm tired

3D LIVING PICTURES

KS1/2 OBJECTIVE	DURATION	RESOURCES
Explore any picture, artwork or photograph through a variety of drama strategies	25-45 minutes, depending on which activities are included	Photographs, paintings, illustrations, or other images (see examples on page 23)

Introduction

The use of pictures, photographs and works of art with drama can have a powerful effect on learning. This session describes how to do a whole class activity by displaying a picture on a smart board, or using a laptop projector. Posters or large images are also effective. The activity can also be done in small groups by giving each group separate printed pictures to use, with fewer characters. These can be thematically linked, or a series of pictures from a story. Another idea is to choose a picture that has plenty of activity in it, cut it into pieces and give a different part to each group to work on.

How to choose an image

The image should have as many characters as there are students. You can use illustrations from story books and text books, historical/documentary photos, graphic novels, movie stills or works of art. It's important that there should be some kind of story or subtext which appeals to the students.

TIMING	CONTENT	RESOURCES
5 mins	**BEGINNING** Show the picture to the students and spend a few minutes asking them to look carefully at what is happening in the scene. You can give them speaking prompts, such as *'I can see…', 'I imagine…'* or *'I can hear'*. One really good prompt is *'I wonder'*. For example, you could say *'I wonder where they are going…'* or *'I wonder what is in the boy's parcel.'*	*Selected image (printed or projected)*
5 mins	**CHOOSE A CHARACTER** When students have examined the picture in greater detail, explain that you would like to bring the picture to life. Each student will be asked to choose a character or object from the picture. When the group is ready, ask them to 'step into the picture' one by one. They should stand in front of the picture, explain who they are and make a freeze frame of their chosen character or object as accurately as possible. This is a good way to practise prepositions, for example, *'I am the dog in front of the whale'* or *'I am the blue helicopter above the whale'.*	*Freeze Frames (p. 56)*
5 mins	**THOUGHT TRACKING** To develop the story behind the picture we start with what the characters are thinking, using *Thought Tracking*. Simply tap each student on the shoulder (or point at them). The student should speak as the character, voicing their thoughts or feelings. If the student is portraying an animal or object, they may at first choose to make sounds instead of words. Just ask them something like 'if the helicopter/seagull could talk, what would it say?'	*Thought Tracking (p. 68)*

ARTISTS

Examples of artists who include large numbers of people in their pictures: Bosch, Brueghel, Hogarth, Judy Joel, Lowry, Madox-Brown, Archibald Motley, Renoir, Diego Rivera, Seurat, Steen, and photographers such as Henri Cartier-Bresson and Alex Prager.

Many children's picture books contain useful illustrations for this activity (such as 'The Snail and the Whale' by Julia Donaldson and 'Where's Wally?' by Martin Handford) and you can also use stills from movies and animations.

2 mins	**ACTION CLIP** In *Action Clip*, the scene becomes animated. Clap your hands and ask the participants to come to life - speaking and behaving as their character/object/animal from the picture. Do this for a few seconds with the whole group. With a large group, it's likely you won't hear everything that's said. Even so, it's good fun for the group to come to life for a short time - and you can focus on the details in the next exercise.	*Action Clip* *(p. 54)*
5 mins	**SPOTLIGHT** *Spotlight* is used to focus on different parts of the scene. Walk amongst the students and hold your hand above them as though it is a spotlight shining down. Indicate which characters should come to life and be heard. Choose pairs of students, smaller sub-groups or individuals as appropriate.	*Spotlight* *(p. 62)*
15 mins	**GUESS WHO I AM** This quick guessing game is a simple introduction to *Role Play* and *Hot Seating*. Start by demonstrating to the class. Secretly choose a character from the picture. Speak to them as though you are that character and see if they can guess who you are. Here's an example of a character playing 'hide and seek' in the painting *'Children's Games'* by Pieter Bruegel the Elder. *'Okay you lot, I'll count to 20 and I want you all to hide! I promise I won't peep. And don't all hide in the same place. Off you go! One, two, three...'* You only need to say a few sentences and behave briefly as the character. When the students have guessed who you are, ask them to work in pairs. One partner chooses a person/animal/object from the picture and speaks and acts as that character for the other one to guess. Then it's the other partner's turn to secretly choose another character. When everyone's tried it you can ask pairs to show what they did to the rest of the class. They only have to speak a sentence or two, depending on their proficiency.	*Role Play* *(p. 60)*
	OTHER ACTIVITIES You can easily lead on to other drama activities, such as *Soundscapes*. *Improvisation* works well, with small groups developing a short performance showing characters from the picture interacting, or 'before' and 'after' scenes. Pictures are also worthwhile starting points for developing diary/journalistic, descriptive or narrative writing.	*Soundscapes* *(p. 61)* *Improvisation* *(p. 60)*

BULLYING

KS2 OBJECTIVE	DURATION	RESOURCES
Explore situations which involve bullying, using a range of drama strategies	50-60 minutes	Thumbs up/Thumbs down signs (pp. 70-71)

TIMING	CONTENT	RESOURCES
5 mins	**IMAGINARIUM** Ask the students to stand in a circle and think for a few moments of a shape to make with their body (a *Freeze Frame*) related to bullying. It could be a bully, someone who is being bullied or a bystander. Clap your hands for them to make the image. Invite individuals to step into the space one at a time to make their image. They should relate to other characters in the space so that a scene is slowly developed. It's not essential for everybody to step in.	*Imaginarium (p. 58)* *Freeze Frames (p. 56)*
5 mins	**THOUGHT TRACKING** When the scene is sufficiently developed, *Thought Tracking* can be used to establish more about the characters. Tap students on the shoulder and ask them to speak their thoughts aloud. Ask the observers standing around the scene what they think might be happening and where the scene could be taking place. There is room for different interpretations.	*Thought Tracking (p. 68)*
5 mins	**FLASHBACK/FLASH FORWARDS** Explain to those standing in the space that when you clap your hands, you would like them to move silently in slow motion to where they think their character would have been a few moments before. If you wish, you can thought-track the characters again. Now ask them to return to their original positions (the present moment) and then to 'flash forwards' – moving silently in slow-motion – to show what might happen next. Using this technique you have created a story with a beginning, middle and end and can develop it in any number of ways, for example, discussion, hot-seating, role-play and writing.	
10 mins	**ROLE PLAY** Divide the class into small groups and ask them to develop a short scene which could have happened before the invented story. It should involve at least one of the characters from the previous exercises and can be about an argument, peer-pressure or a problem at school or home. Each group can develop their own interpretation of the story. Encourage them to rehearse their ideas.	*Role Play (p. 60)*
10 mins	**BEST BITS** This technique enables all the groups to share their ideas in a short space of time. The groups must decide on one important moment in their story and make a freeze frame to show what is happening at that point. Ask each group in turn to make their freeze frame. When you clap your hands they should bring the freeze frame to life for a few moments so that they can share the dramatic moment from their story.	*Best Bits (p. 54)*

10 mins	**HOT SPOTTING**	*Hot Spotting (p. 57)*

This activity is a variation on *Hot Seating*. Once each of the 'best bits' has been brought to life, you have the opportunity to find out more about the characters and their story. Choose groups which have created a clear dramatic moment and ask them to make their freeze frame again. Use thought tracking with some of the characters. Then encourage the audience to ask the characters relevant questions. Students should stay in their frozen position until they are asked a question.

10 mins	**WHERE DO YOU STAND?**	*Thumbs up/ Thumbs down cards (pp. 70-71)*

This activity enables pupils to explore their own opinions and understand how others feel about bullying. Set up two chairs with 'Agree' and 'Disagree' signs on them (or Thumbs up/Thumbs down signs). Read out one of the following statements at a time and ask the children to place themselves between the signs according to what they believe, stressing that there is not always a 'right' answer. Students standing near each other can discuss their decisions and children can be randomly chosen to explain why they've chosen their particular location. Following this, students can move position if they have formed a new opinion.

Where Do You Stand? (p. 69)

Example statements:
- It's best to keep quiet if you're bullied
- If you see somebody in trouble you should try to stop the bullies
- It's okay to call someone a name if you're only joking
- It's better to tell a friend about bullying than to tell the teacher
- If you ignore bullies they will go away
- Anyone can be a bully
- We can do something about bullying by talking about it
- I know and understand the school policy on bullying

HIT THE HEADLINES

KS1/KS2 OBJECTIVE	DURATION	RESOURCES
Generate ideas for writing a detective/thriller story (or any other genre)	45-60 minutes, can be spread over two or more sessions	Newspaper headlines (pp. 28-29) printed out - at least one per five students. Optional: cameras, notebooks, paper and pens

TIMING	CONTENT	RESOURCES
10 mins	**TEN SECOND OBJECTS** In small groups, students explore ideas in the chosen genre by using their bodies to create objects. For a detective story, give them ten seconds to make objects related to the theme, such as a police car, magnifying glass, camera, handcuffs, prison cell and clue (the group can decide what kind of clue to make, for example, a broken window, a fingerprint or a murder weapon).	*Ten Second Objects (p. 66)*
5 mins	**IMAGINARIUM** Write up or display one of the headlines on pages 28-29 (or make up one of your own). Standing in a circle, read out the chosen headline and ask participants to step in as an object or character related to it. As players step in they should try to relate to others in the scene if possible. For example, one could be a museum guard, one might be a statue, one could be broken glass and another might be a rock thrown through a window. Another example for a murder mystery: participants could be a dead body, a pool of blood, a detective, a grandfather clock and a magnifying glass. Random objects and characters are useful to provide additional narrative choices. When the scene has been created you can ask participants to add adjectives or a descriptive phrase, for example, *'I am a clever but forgetful detective'* or *'I am a smeared fingerprint on the window'*.	*Headline on display* *Imaginarium (p. 58)*
5 mins	**ACTION CLIP** Ask those within the scene and those observing what kind of story may be taking place. How are the objects and characters related to each other? Next, you can choose names for the characters. Using *Action Clip* ask the players to bring the scene to life for a few moments when you clap your hands - and then freeze again. By now a story should be starting to take shape. It's a good idea to take a few photos from different angles - this can be done by yourself or by students in role as forensic photographers.	*Action Clip (p. 54)* *Cameras/devices*
5 mins	**THOUGHT TRACKING** Thought track some of the characters and objects. Ask questions like: What can you see/hear? Where are you going? How do you feel? Who do you believe?	*Thought Tracking (p. 68)*

10 mins plus	**WRITING ACTIVITIES** From here you can proceed to short written activities, for example: – Work in pairs/small groups to write paragraphs of the class story – Write a story sentence on a strip of till roll, then rearrange these to tell the story – Write a news bulletin or headline in a notebook – Tell the story from the point of view of one of the characters/objects – Journalist interviews in pairs	*Pens/pencils* *Writing materials e.g. Till roll or Reporters' Notebooks*
15-20 mins	**HEADLINE STORIES** Divide the class into groups of 5-6. Using *Freeze Frames*, each group must devise a photograph to accompany a new headline. They should spend five minutes discussing ideas for the story and then choose a dramatic moment on which to base their devised photograph. When the groups are ready, they can share their work. Those watching can try to guess the headline before it is revealed. The teacher can use *Thought Tracking* and *Action Clip* if the meaning of the image is unclear.	*Printed headlines (pp. 28-29)* *Freeze Frames (p. 56)* *Action Clip (p. 54)*
	EXTENSION ACTIVITIES In addition to the written activities above, there are opportunities for many other activities based on the devised stories: **Drama** – Interview or *Hot Seat* suspects and other characters – Devise additional *Freeze Frames* to show other moments from the story – Devise and perform a TV reconstruction of the story – Play script (writing and performance) – Video, podcast or radio play **Writing** – News report (for different newspaper audiences) – CSI note books containing notes and drawings of clues – List of clues in each scene – List of suspects – Evidence board – Mind maps – Character descriptions – Wanted poster – Forensic report	*Hot Seating (p. 56)*

PHOTOCOPIABLES

Over the page you will find photocopiable headline suggestions to use with this unit

HOLD THE FRONT PAGE

Headlines can also be used to explore themes from current news, history and fiction:

Fairytales: 'Granny Gets Wolfed Down', 'Should Jack Go Back?', 'Oh Crumbs, Children Lost!' 'Is This Your Shoe?'

History: 'Explorer Finds Mummy', 'Samuel Takes A Peep', 'Queen NOT Amused', 'Small Step or Giant Leap?'

Greek Myths: 'He's Got The Magic Touch', 'Monster is A-Maze-ing', 'Don't Open The Box!' 'Icky Mess for Icarus'

Shakespeare: 'Ship Vanishes in Magic Storm', 'Star-Crossed Tragedy', 'Queen Falls in Love With Donkey'

SNEAKY ROBBERS LOCKED
INSIDE MUSEUM

BALD DETECTIVE FINDS
HAIRY CLUE

SCHOOL CARETAKER
STUCK IN CUPBOARD

SLIPPERY THIEVES
STEAL SOAP

KIDNAPPER LEAVES MESSAGE
ON FRIDGE

MYSTERY BOOK THIEF
STRIKES AGAIN

HEADLINE STORIES (p. 27)

Photocopiable © Drama Resource 2021

CORGI KIDNAPPED IN BUCKINGHAM PALACE

DINOSAUR DISCOVERED IN DUMP

HISTORY LESSONS IN HAUNTED CLASSROOM

STUDENTS LOVE THEIR ALIEN TEACHER

PIRATE TREASURE UNCOVERED IN PLAYGROUND

HAS ANYONE LOST THIS GIRAFFE?

THE LOST AND FOUND CAT

KS1/KS2 OBJECTIVE
Explore the real-life story of a refugee family and their cat using storytelling, discussion and drama

DURATION
75-90 minutes, can be spread over two sessions

RESOURCES
The story is told clearly in this beautifully-illustrated book, which can be used to accompany the lesson: Kuntz, D. and Shrodes, A. (2019). *Lost and Found Cat.* Dragonfly Books. ISBN 978-1524715502

INTRODUCTION

Sura and her family fled Iraq and became refugees in Europe. They took their cat with them, but he became lost during the journey. Following intervention from aid-workers and communities across the world, the family and their pet were reunited. This drama unit explores the challenges faced by the family and other refugees through the heart-warming story of Kunkush, the refugee cat.

There are many accounts of this true story available on the internet. A two-minute video by The Guardian shows Kunkush being reunited with his family. It is generally appropriate for children (but please watch first to check for suitability). This should be shown at the end of the activities.

Guardian video: https://youtu.be/05K-YUezBKA

Websites offering resources for teaching about refugees include UNESCO, Action Aid, Christian Aid, British Red Cross, Amnesty and Oxfam.

PREPARATION

Read the story in advance, and watch the video. You should familiarise yourself with Amy's story in the section 'Teacher in Role'.

My version of the story is included as part of the lesson plan so that you don't need to refer to the book. However, the powerful illustrations and documentary photographs in the book help to bring the story to life and can be shown alongside the storytelling.

TIMING	CONTENT	RESOURCES
2 mins	**STORYTELLING** Tell Part 1 of the story to the class: This is the true story of a refugee cat called Kunkush. He was a big cat with long white fur. It all began in November 2015, when a woman called Sura and her five children had to escape from the war in Iraq. They contacted some people who would help them. The family were only allowed to take two bags, so they packed one bag with food and water and hid their cat inside a basket! When it was dark, they sneaked out and got into a smuggler's car. They hoped Kunkush would keep quiet, otherwise they would have to pay for an extra ticket. When they had driven out of the city they were met by another smuggler. For three days and nights they trudged through forests and mountains, making sure they kept the basket hidden. Luckily, Kunkush kept quiet most of the time. When they slept amongst the trees, they secretly let him out to play.	*Optional: 'Lost and Found Cat' book*

15 mins	**THROUGH THE MOUNTAINS**	*Freeze Frames (p. 56)*

Divide the class into groups of five or six. Explain that they will be making *Freeze Frames* to show different parts of the story, but they will only have ten seconds to make each one. Ask them to show you each image one by one:

Show me:

1.   The family packing two bags for their journey
2.   Sura and the children squashed inside the car
3.   The smuggler, the family and Kunkush walking through the mountains
4.   The children and the cat secretly playing in the forest

When the groups have made their freeze frames, invite them to share with each other. Discuss how groups have shown the scene in similar or different ways. Encourage students to look at how different levels have been used – low, medium and high.

To deepen the learning, for each of the freeze frames pick two or more of the groups to do some quick *Thought Tracking*. You can ask characters questions such as:

– Who are you with?
– What can you see?
– What are you afraid of?
– What do you hope for?
– How can you help?

Use *Action Clip* to bring freeze frames to life for a few moments.

Thought Tracking (p. 68)

Action Clip (p. 54)

3 mins	**STORYTELLING**

Tell Part 2 of the story to the class:

After three exhausting days in the mountains, the family went on a long bus journey to the ancient city of Istanbul in Turkey. They moved from apartment to apartment, always keeping an eye out for the police. Soon it was time to catch a bus to the coast. They couldn't believe their eyes when they saw the boat that would take them to a Greek island. It was just a big rubber dinghy. Sixty people squeezed on board. They set off, but massive waves hit the boat and it started sinking. They quickly returned to the shore. Somehow they managed to keep Kunkush safe and dry.

The family didn't give up. They stayed on board until the boat set off again, this time with fewer people. They bobbed up and down all the way across the sea. Kunkush's basket was broken but he was still safe. Eventually they arrived on the island of Lesbos, where they were met by volunteer aid-workers. The workers helped everyone get through the waves onto the beach. Sura's son Hakam carried the cat basket ashore and went back to help his mother through the waves. But when they returned to the beach, the basket was empty – Kunkush had escaped!

5 mins	**ON THE BOAT**

In the same groups ask them to show you this image as a freeze frame:

– Kunkush and his family on the boat travelling to Lesbos

The following image can be made by the whole class working in silence together to create one big freeze frame.

– Aid-workers helping people from the boat scramble onto the beach in Lesbos

Give the students guidance as they find places in the image; the boat, travellers, aid workers wading through the surf and people helping them onto the beach.

TIMING	CONTENT	RESOURCES
10 mins	**WHAT HAPPENS NEXT?** *In your groups, talk about what you think happened next in the story then make a freeze frame to show your ideas.* When the groups are ready to share their finished freeze frames with each other, you can use any of these drama strategies to explore their ideas: – Thought Tracking – Action Clip – Hot Spotting	*Thought Tracking (p. 68)* *Action Clip (p. 54)* *Hot Spotting (p. 57)*
1 min	**STORYTELLING** Tell Part 3 of the story to the class: **The family looked everywhere for Kunkush. They called out for him, but he was nowhere to be found. They were so upset, but eventually had to carry on their journey without him. Meanwhile Kunkush prowled around until he found a place near the harbour where lots of other cats were looking for fish and crumbs of food near the cafés. They looked thin and hungry. But the cats didn't like Kunkush. They wanted all the food for themselves.** **Eventually Amy, one of the aid-workers, noticed the bedraggled white cat and took him home.**	
10 mins	**MEETING AMY** In this part you will play the role of Amy, the aid-worker. Sit the class in front of a chair. Explain that the children are going to meet Amy. Then turn around and put on a raincoat or hat to denote the character. Sit down as Amy and go through the following information through question and answer: – You have come to tell the children about a cat that you found – You've been working as an aid-worker in Lesbos for three months. (You don't have much time to talk as you have to get back to work soon) – Boats of refugees are arriving all the time, day and night – There's a big and overcrowded refugee camp. Do they know what refugee camps are like? – You were serving soup to other aid-workers near the beach when you noticed a new white cat on its own. It was being bullied by the other cats – Some of the other aid-workers told you that a family had been looking for their cat. You asked around but couldn't find out where the family were – You decided to call the cat *Dias* – the Greek name for Zeus – You've made friends with the cat and taken him home to look after him – Dias has very matted and dirty long fur and you think he might have worms or infections – Explain that you've never looked after a cat before. Does anyone know how you should be looking after him? (Later, Amy took the cat to a vet – see Part 4 below) – Can the children think of ways to help you find the family? (They may suggest a poster campaign or posting online) – Discuss how any publicity will have to be written in different languages, for example, English, Greek, Arabic – Finally explain that you (Amy) have to go back to work.	*Teacher in Role (p. 65)*

Meeting Amy (continued)

Other background information you can include:

- Amy had been travelling in Europe on a sabbatical in 2015 and had witnessed thousands of refugees escaping from conflict. She made contact with a photo-journalist called Doug Kuntz, who helped her find a placement as a volunteer in Lesbos.

Take your leave as Amy and then, returning as the teacher, explain that Amy has gone now. Did the children learn more about Kunkush? You can ask them to summarise points for you as if you didn't know what Amy told them.

Explain what happened next in Part 4:

Amy took Kunkush to the vet, who shaved off most of his fur and gave him injections. Amy looked after Dias for a month while she continued to work as a volunteer. Michelle (Amy's best friend back home in Oklahoma City in the USA) helped her put together a social media campaign.

PUBLICITY CAMPAIGN (OPTIONAL)

Students can be encouraged to devise a publicity campaign to help find Kunkush. They can make flyers, posters and even drawings of Facebook pages – but they should refer to him as *'Dias'* at this point, as that was his name on Lesbos.

THE LOST AND FOUND CAT CONTINUES...

TIMING	CONTENT	RESOURCES
2 mins	**STORYTELLING** Tell Part 5 of the story to the class: **Meanwhile the family left Lesbos, but no-one knew where they had gone. People around the world gave money through the Facebook page to help Dias get better and to assist Amy's campaign. Dias was famous!** **Amy thought Sura and her family might be living in Germany so she took Dias there. He was temporarily adopted by Emma and Simon, a British couple who continued to look for his owners. Then one day, Sura's eldest daughter Rihab saw a photo of Dias on the internet. She was sure it was Kunkush. She could speak some English by now so was able to contact Amy and Michelle. She explained that her family was living in Norway, not Germany. She was put in contact with Emma and Simon in Germany. The family made a Skype call and couldn't believe their eyes when they saw Kunkush on their computer screen. Kunkush could hear them calling his name and looked behind the computer to try and find them.**	
10-15 mins	**SKYPE CALL (IMPROVISATION)** Again working in groups, two children play the parts of Emma and Simon, one person can be Kunkush and the others are Sura's family. They should improvise an online conversation to work out what to do next. You can ask groups to share their improvisations to see what ideas they came up with.	*Improvisation (p. 60)*
2 mins	**STORYTELLING** Tell the final part of the story to the class: **Amy's friend Doug (the photo-journalist) offered to take Kunkush from Germany to Norway to reunite him with his family. Doug arrived in Norway at Sura's new home, carrying Kunkush in a basket. When he arrived, there were TV crews and reporters from around the world, gathered to record the event. Sura and her five children were overwhelmed to see their dear cat after his 4,000 km journey through forests, mountains, cities, sea and air.** **Doug and Amy decided to write a book all about the incredible journey of the cat and his family. They called it 'Lost and Found Cat'. Some money from the book goes to Kunkush's family and some of it goes to help a charity called Médecins Sans Frontières (Doctors Without Borders), which helps to bring medical aid to people in need.**	
3 mins	**SHOW THE VIDEO** - Show *The Guardian* video of Kunkush being reunited with his family - (Scan the QR code to watch the video on YouTube) - You may want to read the subtitles aloud	
5 mins	**DISCUSSION** - What drama strategies did the students use to explore the story? - Were students surprised by the story? - The success of the campaign depended on people working together: Which people on the journey helped in a big or small way to return Kunkush to his family? - Why do people work as volunteers to help refugees? - Is there anything we can do to help refugees?	

REFUGEE RUCKSACK

KS2 OBJECTIVE
Explore what we really value when we take a journey and find out what actual refugees took with them on their travels

DURATION
20-30 minutes

RESOURCES
Masking tape or chalk to mark out the shape of a rucksack or suitcase on the floor

Web page to show at end: https://medium.com/uprooted/what-s-in-my-bag-758d435f6e62

TIMING	CONTENT	RESOURCES
5 mins	**DISCUSSION** *In pairs discuss and write down: If you had to leave home because of an earthquake, flooding, or war, which six objects would you want to take with you?* You can show an image from '*The Arrival*' to inspire children's ideas (*page 3*, the husband and wife closing the suitcase together).	*Tan, S. (2007). 'The Arrival'. Hodder. ISBN: 978-0734415868*
5 mins	**DISCUSSION** *Join with another pair and share your thoughts.* *Imagine you are going to live in a refugee camp a long way away. If the four of you were sharing a rucksack and could only put in one object each, what would it be?*	
5 mins	**PACKING THE RUCKSACK** Mark out the shape of a suitcase or rucksack on the floor. The class should make a circle around the rucksack. *Just imagine you have to leave home tomorrow. We need to decide what to pack in this rucksack for a long journey to a new country.* *If you have an idea, put your hand up and step in as an object that you think should be packed. You can make an object on your own or with a friend. Make the shape of the object and say what you are.* Allow children to step into the shape until there is no space left. There may still be children watching, who have not stepped in.	*Masking tape or chalk* *Speaking Objects (p. 62)*
5 mins	**JUSTIFY YOUR CHOICE** Through mime, show the children that you're trying to close the rucksack. *Oh dear, I don't think I can fit everything in. Can any of the objects explain to me why I should pack them?* Tap children on the shoulder (or point to them) and ask them to justify why they should be packed. For example, they might say '*You should take me because I will keep you dry when it rains*' or '*If you pack me, I will charge your phone.*' When each object has justified why it should be taken, you can ask children watching if they think any object could be removed. When one or two objects have been removed, you can mime that the rucksack can now be closed.	
10 mins	**DISCUSSION** Show the web page by scanning the QR code or visiting the link above. The web page introduces some refugees, the bags they travelled with and the precious items they decided to bring. These thought-provoking photos can lead onto further discussion and research about refugees and human rights.	

SCIENCE AND DRAMA   1

INTRODUCTION

This section covers a range of ideas for exploring science through drama. The activities can be used to enliven science lessons, as revision or to test prior knowledge before embarking on a topic. With adaptation, the ideas can be used with a range of ages. The activities can be extended by combining with each other and with other drama games.

TIMING	SOURCES OF LIGHT	RESOURCES
10 mins	**AIM: IDENTIFY OBJECTS THAT MAKE OR REFLECT LIGHT** *Imaginarium* is a very easy game to play and can be used to explore or revise many scientific topics. Here's how to use it to explore *Sources of Light*. A range of other topics are suggested below. Begin with the students standing in a large circle. Ask them to step forward one at a time as an object that is a source of light. They should make the shape of the object and say what they are, for example, *'I am a firefly'*. Students can step in with a partner if they think of an object they can make together. Once you have plenty of suggestions, say *'Whoosh!'* to clear the space. **Variations** – Step in as natural or man-made sources of light – Step in as an object that generates or reflects light – Ask students to add an adjective when you tap them on the shoulder, e.g. *'I am a flickering torch'* **Useful Adjectives** blazing, blinding, bright, clear, cool, dazzling, dim, electric, flashing, flickering, fluorescent, glimmering, glistening, glittering, glowing, golden, harsh, reflected, shimmering, shining, soft, sparkly, twinkling, wavering, white, yellow	*Imaginarium (p. 58)*

TIMING	IMAGINARIUM - THEMES TO EXPLORE	RESOURCES
10 mins or more	**AIM: USE IMAGINARIUM TO REPRESENT OR EXPLORE:** – *Habitats.* Select an environment (such as a woodland or pond) and students step in as animals and plants which would be found there – *Food chains.* Continuing from the previous theme, ask students to move closer to creatures to which they are related in a food chain – *Carnivores/herbivores/omnivores* – *Solar system.* Students step in as planets, moons, comets and asteroids. Add in movement while playing the *Planets Suite* by Holst – *Materials.* Step in as objects made of wood, plastic, metal, glass or rock. Play again to explore objects with different properties e.g. sharp, transparent, stretchy, man-made, heavy, rough, bendy, shiny, waterproof, floating/sinking – *The human circulatory system.* Add in movement to demonstrate the functions of the heart, blood vessels and blood – *Human digestive system.* Can they put the parts in order? – *Eco-systems.* Small groups are each given a different eco-system to devise, such as the Arctic or Sahara desert, then the others watch and guess – *Electrical circuits.* Students represent switches, batteries, bulbs, buzzers etc.	*Imaginarium (p. 58)*

TIMING	THE WATER CYCLE	RESOURCES
25 mins	**AIM: PERFORM THE WATER CYCLE**	*Display your own description of the water cycle*

AIM: PERFORM THE WATER CYCLE

Divide the class into small groups. Set a time limit of 5-10 minutes to devise a short movement sequence showing the water cycle. Play music while the students are practising or while they perform to each other.

Sequence

- Ice
- Ice melts into water
- Water evaporates into vapour
- Vapour cools and condenses into clouds
- Rain falls
- Water freezes once more

TIMING	LIFE CYCLES	RESOURCES
25 mins		

AIM: PERFORM THE LIFE-CYCLE OF AN ANIMAL OR PLANT

- This activity can be used to devise performances for presentation in assembly

Divide the class into small groups. Give each group a card with the description/ diagram of an animal or plant life-cycle. Set a time limit (e.g. 7 minutes) for the groups to rehearse a short presentation as though it is a video on YouTube. You may prefer to give all groups the same life-cycle to work on.

Example life-cycles: butterfly, chicken, dragonfly, frog, human, mustard seed, oak tree, sunflower

Variations

- One student is the narrator and the others perform the video, becoming whatever is needed, whether it is cells, animals, plants or other objects
- The groups dance/mime their scene to music
- Devise a series of *Freeze Frames* and move in slow-motion from one frame to the next
- Two groups perform at the same time for comparison of plants/animals

Resources:
Life-cycle cards (plants and animals) (p. 42)

You Tubers (p. 46)

Freeze Frames (p. 56)

TIMING	FOUR SEASONS	RESOURCES
10-15 mins		*Best Bits (p. 54)*

AIM: DESCRIBE WEATHER ASSOCIATED WITH THE SEASONS

In small groups, prepare a TV weather forecast going through the months of the year or the seasons. One person will be the presenter while the others act out the weather being described, or typical activities for the climate. Groups can swap presenters if they want to share the narration.

Variations

- Add vocal/body sound effects
- Perform to music

Teaching Tip

Save time when groups present their work by using *Best Bits*.

SCIENCE AND DRAMA   2

TIMING	BODY PARTS GAME	RESOURCES

10 mins

AIM: RECOGNISE AND MATCH PARTS OF THE BODY

Person to Person

This is a fun warm-up game for the whole class. Students walk around the space making the sound of an animal (e.g. clucking like a chicken). When you call out 'Person to person,' everybody finds a partner. Now call out the name of one or more parts of the body which the students have to connect e.g. 'Elbow to knee'.

This can be interpreted in any way they like e.g. they touch an elbow to an elbow and a knee to a knee, or they each touch an elbow to a knee. The more creative, the better; flatter them for coming up with ingenious ways to link.

Name another pair of body parts to match with their partners before they move around on their own as an animal. You can change animals each time, so they could be oinking like a pig or squeaking like a mouse. Call out 'Person to person' again for them to find a new partner and match more body parts.

Body part examples

– Finger to nose, back to back, big toe to ear, shin to chin, palm to ankle, knuckles to chin, little finger to shoulder blade, knees to knees

Animal sounds

– Baa like a sheep, moo like a cow, neigh like a horse, quack like a duck

Variations

– Call out a number; they get into groups of that number then you ask them to connect (for example) 7 fingers, 2 chins and 6 wrists
– Older students can be challenged with anatomical terms such as 'scapula to humerus' or 'skull to vertebra'

RESOURCES

Ankle
Arm
Back
Big toe
Bottom
Calf
Cheek
Chin
Ear
Elbow
Finger
Foot
Hand
Head
Knee
Knuckle
Leg
Palm
Neck
Nose
Shin
Shoulder

TIMING	PHOTOSYNTHESIS	RESOURCES

25 mins

AIM: PERFORM THE PROCESS OF PHOTOSYNTHESIS

Give small groups a card each showing one of the following aspects of photosynthesis. Give groups 5-10 minutes to devise a short movement sequence based on their card. When they are ready, show the images in order.

Sequence

1. Plants need air, sunlight, water and nutrients to be healthy
2. The roots of a plant keep it steady and upright in the soil; they anchor the plant
3. The root hairs of a plant take up water from the soil and carry it to the leaves
4. The stem carries water and nutrients to different parts of the plant
5. Plants absorb carbon dioxide from the air through small holes (stomata) in the leaves
6. Leaves use light from the sun, along with carbon dioxide and water to make glucose and oxygen
7. Oxygen is released into the air through holes in the leaves (stomata) and glucose is carried around the plant
8. Leaves contain chlorophyll (which makes them green) and they are flat to help them absorb sunlight

Photosynthesis cards (p. 43)

Optional: Music to play while students perform their pieces

TIMING	GLOBAL WARMING: PROBLEMS AND SOLUTIONS	RESOURCES

25 mins

AIM: CONSIDER GLOBAL WARMING PROBLEMS AND SOLUTIONS

Use *3D Living Pictures* to explore a photograph of an environment affected by global warming e.g. deforested area in rainforest, melting glaciers, Californian wild fires, Great Barrier Reef. Working with the whole class, students step into the space to represent objects and creatures that may live in the location, including anything that may be unseen in the photo, such as insects.

Use *Thought Tracking* or *Hot Seating* to find out what the objects/creatures know about the problem and how they feel about the situation.

Divide the class into groups and ask them to devise a freeze frame showing a potential solution to the problem. Share these and discuss whether the solution is realistically achievable.

Variations

- Give out different photos to small groups. Give them time to prepare a *3D Living Picture* then share it with the rest of the class, who can guess the environment and thought track students

Resources:
Photograph(s) of the effects of global warming

3D Living Pictures (p. 22)

Thought Tracking (p. 68)

Hot Seating (p. 56)

Action Clip (p. 54)

TIMING	GLOBAL WARMING: ATTITUDES	RESOURCES

15 mins

AIM: EXPLORE ATTITUDES AND KNOWLEDGE OF GLOBAL WARMING

Where Do You Stand? is a fast and effective way of discovering everybody's opinions about a subject. Set up two chairs with signs on them saying 'Agree' and 'Disagree' or Thumbs up/Thumbs down signs.

Read out any of the following statements one by one and ask students to choose a place to stand in relation to the Agree/Disagree signs. The nearer they stand to one of the chairs, the stronger the opinion they're expressing. Those who don't know, are open-minded or don't want to say can move towards the middle.

Once they have chosen a position you can spotlight a range of attitudes by asking individuals why they chose to stand in a particular place. After a few views have been gathered, give students the opportunity to change their position if they want.

Statements

- Rainforests are the biggest preventers of climate change
- Cows' burps are a major cause of climate change
- Weather is the same as climate
- Electric cars are good for the natural world
- Going vegan helps to improve the climate
- Paddling a canoe to school (or riding a bike) would help the environment
- I recycle things more than five times every day
- The last twenty years have been the warmest ones on record
- Climate change is bad for polar bears and other animals
- Climate change causes daffodils to bloom at the wrong time of year
- I do at least one thing every day to help prevent climate change
- I know how to reduce my carbon footprint
- I understand how recycling helps to slow climate change

Resources:
Printed signs showing 'Agree'/'Disagree' or Thumbs up/Thumbs down signs (pp. 70-71)

Where Do You Stand? (p. 69)

SCIENCE AND DRAMA 3

TIMING	WHO'S FOR BREAKFAST?	RESOURCES

10 mins

AIM: EXPLORE FOOD, MEALS AND HEALTHY EATING

Mark out a circular shape (like a plate or bowl) in the centre of the space. Everybody stands around the 'plate'. Explain the rules of *Imaginarium*.

Announce a meal time e.g. breakfast/lunch/dinner/tea

- Students step in one at a time as an item of food they think is suited to the meal
- They say what they are and make the shape of the food item
- When the plate is full or you have a balanced meal, say *'Whoosh!'* to clear the space and start again

Using this method you can explore a variety of themes:

- Step in as favourite food/meat/fruit/vegetables
- Healthy/unhealthy food
- Carbohydrates, proteins, fats
- Vegan/vegetarian/gluten free
- Foods containing minerals/vitamins
- Ingredients for a recipe e.g. chocolate cookies, mixed salad, pizza

Variation

Divide into small groups. Each group prepares a type of meal. Show each group and ask the others to guess the meal/food items.

Resources:
Masking tape/ chalk

Imaginarium (p. 58)

TIMING	ANIMAL HABITATS	RESOURCES

15 mins

AIM: EXPLORE AND COMPARE ANIMAL HABITATS

Mime/movement: Students find a space. Name an animal and ask them to move around the space as that animal.

Explore different ways of moving. Stop in a new location on your own. Imagine you are in the creature's home. Where do you think it lives? Is it under a stone, in the rainforest, on the seashore, in water? Explore your home; is it deep or shallow, wide or narrow?

Depending on students' pre-existing knowledge, you can give them further details about the habitat. Perhaps they should dig a tunnel, hide under coral, explore the hive or build a nest. Repeat with other animals and habitats.

Variations

- Give out cards with names of different animals and their habitats. Students first explore their animal movement and habitat through mime, as above. Next, they are paired with a different 'animal' and each has to show their partner round their home (using speech and movement). These improvisations can be shared with the class
- TV Show: Working in pairs, prepare an improvisation where one of you is a TV presenter and the other is an animal showing the visitor around their 'crib' and perhaps inviting the visitor to a tasty meal!

Example Animals

Angelfish, ant, bat, bee, camel, crab, elephant, fox, frog, hedgehog, kangaroo, otter, parrot, penguin, pig, rabbit, sloth, stick insect, stork, whale, woodlouse

Resources:
Animal/habitat printed cards (pp. 44-45)

Improvisation (p. 60)

TIMING	WALK ON THE WILD SIDE	RESOURCES
10-15 mins	**AIM: OBSERVE AND APPRECIATE THE NATURAL ENVIRONMENT** This outdoors activity can be done as part of a nature walk or scavenger hunt. During the walk, ask students to carefully observe the trees, plants, insects and animals. While you are still outside, play *Imaginarium* as a large group or use *Freeze Frames* in smaller groups to create representations of different parts of the environment or individual plants and creatures. *Soundscape:* Sit the children down, ask them to close their eyes and listen to the sounds around them. Discuss what they heard as well as any other sounds they think will be found in the natural environment. Conduct a soundscape, with children making the sounds they have heard. They can also do this back in the classroom to remind them of their visit.	*Imaginarium (p. 58)* *Freeze Frames (p. 56)* *Soundscapes (p. 61)*

TIMING	EXPLORER'S RUCKSACK	RESOURCES
15 mins	**AIM: CHOOSE EQUIPMENT FOR DIFFERENT ENVIRONMENTS** **Preparation:** Mark a larger-than-life outline of a rucksack on the floor with masking tape or chalk. **Imaginarium** The class makes a circle around the rucksack outline. Explain that this is a rucksack for an explorer. Ask students to make up a name for the explorer. Explain that the students have been chosen as special advisors to decide what to pack for an expedition to the South Pole. – One at a time, students step into the shape as an object that they think should be packed. They can make an object on their own or with a friend – When a few students have stepped in, use *Thought Tracking* to question 'objects' why they think they should be packed – Are they suitable for the climate? – This can lead on to discussion of thermal insulators **Variation** Divide into small groups. Each group is given a card with the name/picture of a different environment. Their task is to decide on a list of equipment to pack in a rucksack for a journey to that destination. They can plan this through drawing and writing and follow it up with a performance where each object explains why it has been packed. **Example Environments and Journeys** Amazon rainforest, Antarctica, Egyptian pyramids, Everglades, Galapagos Islands, Himalayas, hot air balloon, Machu Picchu, Mars, the Moon, Sahara desert, Siberia, submarine voyage, underground caves, Victoria Falls, volcano	*Masking tape/ chalk* *Environment/ Journey cards (pp. 46-47)* *Imaginarium (p. 58)* *Thought Tracking (p. 68)*

TIMING	PACK A PICNIC	RESOURCES
10-15 mins	**AIM: EXPLORE UNDERSTANDING OF HEALTHY FOOD** Using the approach above, mark out the shape of a picnic hamper. Students have to step into the hamper showing healthy foods to pack for a picnic. After doing the activity as a whole class, students can work in smaller groups to plan a tasty, healthy and nutritionally balanced picnic through writing and drawing. **Variation** – Use the same game to make a vegetarian, vegan or gluten-free picnic	*Masking tape/ chalk*

Butterfly	Chicken
Dragonfly	Frog
Human	Mustard Seed
Oak Tree	Sunflower

1

Plants need air, sunlight, water and nutrients to be healthy

2

The roots of a plant keep it steady and upright in the soil; they anchor the plant

3

The root hairs of a plant take up water from the soil and carry it to the leaves

4

The stem carries water and nutrients to different parts of the plant

5

Plants absorb carbon dioxide from the air through small holes (stomata) in the leaves

6

Leaves use light from the sun, along with carbon dioxide and water to make glucose and oxygen

7

Oxygen is released into the air through holes in the leaves (stomata) and glucose is carried around the plant

8

Leaves contain chlorophyll (which makes them green) and they are flat to help them absorb sunlight

Angelfish	Ant
Coral Reef	*Nest*

Bat	Elephant
Cave	*Tropical Jungle*

Fox	Frog
Den	*Pond*

Hedgehog	Hermit Crab
Burrow	*Shell*

Honey Bee	Otter
Hive	*Holt*

Parrot	Penguin
Nest	*Land and Sea*

Pig	Sloth
Sty	*Branch*

Stick Insect	Stork
Tree	*Chimney Nest*

EXPLORER'S RUCKSACK (p. 41)

Amazon Rainforest	Antarctica
Egyptian Pyramids	The Everglades
Galapagos Islands	Himalayas
Hot Air Balloon	Machu Picchu

Mars

The Moon

Sahara Desert

Siberia

Submarine Journey

Underground Caves

Victoria Falls

Volcano

A MIDSUMMER NIGHT'S DREAM

KS1/KS2 OBJECTIVE
Become familiar with the setting and characters of 'A Midsummer Night's Dream', culminating in a live performance of the story of Titania and Oberon

DURATION
70-80 minutes, can be spread over two sessions

RESOURCES
Video summary of the play, such as:
RSC Midsummer Night's Dreaming: Billy Trailer (2 minutes)
BBC Shakespeare in Shorts (3.5 mins)
Shakespeare The Animated Tales (25.5 minutes)

TIMING	CONTENT	RESOURCES
10 mins	**INTRODUCE THE PLAY** *Discussion:* Talk briefly about the story of *'A Midsummer Night's Dream'.* Have the students heard of it? Can anyone recall characters or events from the story? An illustrated book or video trailer may be helpful here (see *Resources* above). The idea is to whet the students' appetites, before they learn more about the story and characters. Explain that the class will find out more about the story and act some of it out. Much of the play takes place in an enchanted forest. Ask for suggestions about ways in which actors and directors might create a spooky atmosphere on the stage or in a movie. These could include music, lighting, costume, scenery, storytelling, acting and sound effects.	*Story book or video trailer*
10 mins	**THE ENCHANTED FOREST** **Pair shapes:** Divide the class into pairs. Partners should work together to make the physical shape of any object, character or animal that might be found in an enchanted forest, for example a spooky tree, fish in a stream, magical flower, spider, dragonfly, fairy spirit. Don't limit children to objects and characters from the play - this is a chance to let their imaginations fly. Remember, the characters and objects should be magical! Then tell them: *Let's see if we can create an enchanted forest scene for A Midsummer Night's Dream! We'll do this by playing the game Imaginarium to make a 'stage picture'.* Everybody stands in a circle. Students step in with their partner to make their shapes. They should state what their object is by saying *'I am...'* or *'We are...'* for example, a squirrel eating a magical acorn, a fairy king and queen having an argument, a wizard woodpecker meeting a grasshopper. Objects and characters from different pairs should relate to each other where appropriate. Once the stage picture is completed, you can ask students to describe their character/object with an adjective or sentence when you tap them on the shoulder, or bring the scene to life for a few moments by clapping your hands. When you're finished, wave your hands and say *'Whoosh!'* to clear the space. You can mention any of their characters and objects that are particularly relevant to *'A Midsummer Night's Dream.*	*Imaginarium (p. 58)*
10 mins	**SOUNDSCAPE** *We're going to create the atmosphere of a spooky forest through sound. The human voice is said to be the most flexible and creative musical instrument there is, so what kind of spooky forest sounds can you think of?* Ask students to suggest or make sounds and move onto creating a *soundscape* where you conduct the group to vocally create the atmosphere of the forest. Sounds can include creaky trees, strange voices, thunderclaps, animals and strange music. After trying it once, ask students if they thought it was spooky enough. Could they improve it and do it a second time?	*Soundscapes (p. 61)* *Optional: Sound recorder*

10 mins	**RAINSTORM**	

As preparation for the Whoosh Storytelling, you can practise this optional activity (which will be repeated in the performance). The whole class will create the sound of a rainstorm. Students are asked to carefully follow the movements of the teacher. Start by tapping one finger on the palm of your hand; it sounds just like raindrops. Slowly build the effect by using two, three, four and then five fingers so that everyone is clapping their hands loudly.

When the storm reaches a crescendo, slowly reduce the volume with four, three, two then just one finger again tapping on the palm. You can only really appreciate this charming effect by trying it in a large group.

To extend the activity, when everybody is clapping their hands loudly, you might want to progress onto slapping your thighs, followed by stamping your feet to create a realistic clap of thunder!

10 mins	**STOP, GO, JUMP, CLAP, SHOW ME**	*Stop, Go, Jump, Clap (p. 63)*

This lively activity gives students the chance to become acquainted with characters from the story through a lively game.

Characters (try as many as you wish):

A *brave hero* or *heroine* exploring the forest

Puck - an invisible spirit who can change into any object and is always playing tricks on people. Servant to the fairy king

Oberon - king of all the magical spirits in the woods. Extremely handsome and wise. Clap to summon your servant!

Titania - the gorgeous fairy queen, who falls in love with a donkey!

Cobweb - Titania's servant, so tiny that you can hardly see him/her at all

An enchanted squirrel, owl, frog etc.

Nick Bottom - a vain and proud actor who thinks he deserves an Oscar

Theseus - proud Duke of Athens (he once killed the Minotaur)

A magical flower - used to charm people into falling in love

A MIDSUMMER NIGHT'S DREAM

TIMING	CONTENT	RESOURCES
15 mins	**STORYTELLING WHOOSH** *Now that we know more about the characters, we're going to listen to part of the story of 'A Midsummer Night's Dream' and act it out at the same time.* Ask everybody to stand in a circle, then read out the *Storytelling Whoosh* on the opposite page. When you reach an object or character marked in **bold**, ask one of the students to step into the centre to become that person/object. Move round the circle in order rather than picking students out. Often there will be actions to do or words to repeat, as described in the story (for example, Puck has to collect ingredients for the spell). After each section, say 'Whoosh!' and wave your arms as a signal for students to go back to their original places. Continue the story with the next student in the circle becoming the next object. In this way you can work your way round the whole circle (at least once) so that everyone gets a chance to join in. Before you read the story, teach everyone this magic spell and get them to practise it a couple of times: *'What you see when you awake, will you for your true-love take.'* Of course they must promise never to repeat it outside these four walls!	*Storytelling Whoosh!* (p. 64)
5 mins	**REFLECTION** – Did the students enjoy and understand the story? – Which parts did they enjoy the most? – Which parts were challenging? – Explain that this is only part of the story of *A Midsummer Night's Dream* – there is even more to come!	
	EXTENSION ACTIVITIES – Develop the Whoosh! story into a performance with music, movement and soundscapes – Draw a storyboard or story map of the main events – Rewrite the story in a new setting, for example, under the ocean or in outer space	*Soundscapes* (p. 61)

A MIDSUMMER NIGHT'S DREAM

STORYTELLING WHOOSH!

This is a story of mischievous spirits, a magical flower and donkey ears...

Once upon a time there was an enchanted forest. In the forest were strange and magical **trees - one, two, three**. The leaves of the trees would whisper secret messages to each other in the night. And of course there were the enchanted spirits. **Oberon** was king of all the spirits in the woods. He was extremely handsome and wise. He had a clever servant called **Robin Goodfellow** (also known as Puck), who worked for him throughout the night. Puck (who was a hobgoblin) would bring Oberon delicious food to eat and special ingredients for his magic spells, such as **magical mushrooms, poisonous frogs** or a **hairy spider** *(this can be two children together)*. Puck liked to get up to mischief and played tricks on everyone he met.

The queen of the fairies was called **Titania**. She was so gorgeous that if a man even glanced at her, he would fall in love for ever. One midsummer night, Titania called for her fairy servants. Here are four of them - **Peaseblossom, Cobweb, Moth** and **Mustardseed**. They were so tiny that you could hardly see them at all. They fluttered around on delicate wings to bring Titania whatever she needed - delicious food, fine clothes and fragrant flowers to sleep on. How happy they all were in the enchanted wood.

WHOOSH!

But on this midsummer night something strange happened. You see, **Titania** and her fairies - **Peaseblossom, Cobweb, Mustardseed** and **Moth** - were looking after a beautiful and proud young **Indian prince**. They decided to make him a beautiful crown of flowers. But **Oberon** wished to take the boy away from Titania. He thought the prince could serve him as a brave knight, guarding the enchanted forest. Titania wouldn't let him take her prince, so the king and queen of the fairies had a big argument. Their voices were so loud that the fairies hid under tiny acorn cups. And this is where we need everybody's help *(encourage students to make the rainstorm sound effects)*. The winds blew, the rains fell, the puddles grew deep, the thunder boomed, the forest was flooded and covered in fog.

WHOOSH!

So **Oberon** thought of a clever plan. He summoned his trusty servant **Puck**. *'Fetch me a magic flower,'* said Oberon. Puck flew off to look around the forest. Soon he found the **enchanted flower** (it was a pansy) and brought it back for Oberon.

In another part of the forest, **Titania** was feeling oh-so-tired, so **her fairies - one, two, three, four** sang her a lullaby. *'Lulla-lulla-lullaby'* – that's how it went! She fell fast asleep on her flowery bed and the fairies vanished.

Oberon crept up and squeezed the juice of the flower into Titania's eyes. He whispered *'What you see when you awake, will you for your true-love take.'* (All the students should join in). Oberon and Puck crept behind some **trees**. Nearby were some **actors** practising a play. They were trying hard to remember their lines: *'The raging rocks and shivering shocks...'* One of them was called **Nick Bottom**. He walked behind the trees but he couldn't see the fairies - (obviously, they were invisible). Puck played a trick. He magically turned Bottom's head into the head of a donkey with big long ears! Bottom returned to the other actors and started braying and singing. The actors ran away in fear. At that moment Titania woke up. The first person she saw was Bottom. *'What angel wakes me from my flowery bed?'* she asked.

WHOOSH!

Titania had fallen deeply in love with **Bottom**, even though he had big donkey ears. She summoned her fairies: '**Peaseblossom, Cobweb, Moth** and **Mustardseed**!' They soon came flying in. *'Ready'* they said. Titania told them, *'Bring my love whatever he wants.'* So the fairies brought him apricots and grapes, figs and honey. But he didn't like any of it. What he wanted was oats and hay. Bottom's head was so hairy that it felt really itchy. Two of the fairies scratched his head and the others fanned him with their butterfly wings. Titania tied flowers around his long donkey ears and fed him with dried peas, which made him extremely happy. Soon they all fell fast asleep. Bottom started snoring.

Oberon and **Puck** crept in to watch. Oberon was pleased with the trick they had played and thought that Titania had learned her lesson. He waved his hand to remove the spell from her. *'Awake, my sweet queen,'* he said. Titania woke and took one look at the man with the donkey head. *'What an ugly mug!'* she said. Puck waved his hand and Bottom's donkey head disappeared. Oberon and Titania smiled at each other. They were friends again. At that moment a lark started singing in the trees. It was almost morning! The fairies vanished and Bottom wandered off to find his actor friends.

And that is where our story ends.

WHOOSH!

YOU TUBERS

KS2 OBJECTIVE
Quickly prepare and present a story or information in the form of a 'video' performed live by students

DURATION
30-35 minutes

RESOURCES
Find one or two appropriate videos from YouTube or any other channel, showing how to play a musical instrument, improve football skills, do a magic trick, bake a cake, do a dance or look after a pet

TIMING	CONTENT	RESOURCES
5-10 mins	**WATCH AND DISCUSS** Show the example video(s). Discuss what elements were used to structure the videos e.g. introduction, interviews, demonstrations, real-life or acted scenes, a number of steps, a summary, credits.	*TV or screen to show video*
10 mins	**PREPARATION** Divide the class into groups of about five. Explain that each group will prepare and then perform a short video. There will be at least one presenter and the others will perform, becoming whatever is needed, whether objects, animals or people. – The group should discuss the idea or story and decide who will be the presenter (although this can be shared). They don't need long to rehearse, as part of the fun is seeing them make it up as they go along – Remind them that most videos are quite short and that their video should last between one to two minutes	
15-20 mins	**PERFORMANCE** Each group performs their video, with a strict time-limit of no longer than two minutes.	
	SUGGESTED THEMES – Cooking: One person describes the recipe while the others become ingredients, cooking utensils or people eating the meal. This can be entertaining to watch as students pretend to be ingredients being chopped up, fried and so on – Holiday slide show – Tourist guide to home town/country – Tips for healthy living – How to make friends – How to score a goal – How to carry out a surgical procedure – My lucky day – My unlucky day – Natural history documentary (especially funny if it involves a food chain) – Looking after a pet – Science experiment – History lecture on a famous event – Book or movie review	

DRAMA GAMES
& STRATEGIES

Tip-top drama games and strategies – instructions and teaching tips

ACTION CLIP   Bring freeze frames to life

 7 years +

🕐 **2 minutes per group**

👥 **Small groups**

🎭 **Improvisation**

After creating a *Freeze Frame*, explain that you would like the group to bring the scene alive for a few moments with speech and movement. Initiate this by saying *'Action!'* or clapping your hands.

Let the improvisation run for a short time (before the performers run out of steam) and end it with a signal such as *'Cut!', 'Freeze!'* or by clapping your hands a second time. The improvisation should last for just a few seconds or no longer than half a minute.

Action Clip gives students the opportunity to enjoy acting out a small part of the story without worrying about how to start or finish the scene. The teacher can easily control how much is shown, especially if the students start to repeat themselves or run out of things to say. After a few sessions of working in this way, students will become more and more confident about devising and presenting short scenes.

Optional: Ask students to bring the scene to life in slow-motion
Examples: *The Tiger Child (p. 5), 3D Living Pictures (p. 23), The Lost and Found Cat (p. 32)*
Related: *Freeze Frames, Improvisation, Thought Tracking*

BEST BITS   Quickly share group work

👥 **7 years +**

🕐 **5 minutes**

👥 **Small groups**

🎭 **Improvisation**

When groups develop scenes or improvisations, they inevitably want to show them to the rest of the class. With several groups this can take a while, especially when the mind begins to wander. So when students have finished devising, ask them to choose the 'best bit' of their improvisation and to prepare a *Freeze Frame* of that moment. Then when it's their turn, ask each group to make the freeze frame and use *Action Clip* to bring it to life. That way, everybody gets to show their favourite moments in a much shorter space of time without (literally) losing the plot.

Normally when groups 'perform' a scene, they are actually devising it all over again. In addition, it can be difficult for students to know when to finish an improvisation. And by the time the last group is up, they really have forgotten what they planned. So try *Best Bits* - everyone is a winner!

Examples: *The King's Sentence (p. 18), Bullying (p. 24), Four Seasons (p. 37)*
Related: *Action Clip, Freeze Frames, Improvisation, Thought Tracking*

CONSCIENCE ALLEY   Give advice to characters

- 🚶 **7 years +**
- 🕐 **10-20 minutes**
- 👥 **Whole class**
- 👤 **Decision-making**

A character walks down an alleyway created by members of the class as they use persuasive arguments to help make a decision. This is an effective technique for exploring any kind of dilemma faced by a character, providing an opportunity to analyse a decisive moment in greater detail.

The students form two lines facing each other, a couple of metres apart. One person (the teacher or a student) takes the role of the character making the decision and walks between the lines, as each person speaks their advice. Conscience Alley is often organised so that those on one side give opposing advice to those on the other. When the character reaches the end of the alley, they decide on a course of action, weighing up the advice that has been given.

This drama technique can be applied to a range of subjects across the curriculum, whenever a character is faced with a decision. It may be that you reach a certain point in your drama lesson, or while reading a story aloud, or describing an historical event, when such a moment occurs. Turn the situation around on the students so that they have to consider the issues involved. Then in role as Oliver Twist, Greta Thunberg or the Big Bad Wolf, walk down the Conscience Alley as members of the class whisper their advice to you.

Teaching Tips
- Younger or less confident participants may walk down the alley in pairs
- Those giving advice can also take on roles, such as different characters from a book, or characters related to the theme
- Use prompts, such as 'You should...' or 'If I were you I would...'
- Alternatively, the persuaders can voice the character's thoughts: e.g. 'I should apologise...' or 'I should speak my opinion proudly'

Example: *If Pets Could Speak (p. 15)*
Related: *Where Do You Stand?*

SHOWING OFF

Children need to learn good audience skills. Encourage them to listen and watch carefully when groups are sharing work. Each group can be allocated a 'buddy' group to make comments on.

Encourage students to look at each other's work with a critical but supportive eye. What did they like most? What made the scene or presentation work? What can be improved?

FREEZE FRAMES   Create instant scenes using your body

- **5 years +**
- **5 minutes +**
- **Whole class, small groups and individuals**
- **Improvisation, Movement**

Freeze Frames (also known as 'still images' and 'frozen pictures') provide a fun and accessible starting point to explore or develop a dramatic moment. They're perfect for introducing students to drama as they're simple to make. As there are no lines to learn they can help shyer performers gain confidence.

Freeze frames can be planned and rehearsed in a short time, or made intuitively without discussion. They're effective for communicating ideas and exploring a story or theme. They can be used to represent people, objects and even abstract concepts like emotions.

As no speaking is involved in presenting images, the approach appeals to pupils who are less verbally confident, preparing the ground for *Role Play*. Using the body to make shapes encourages awareness of physical communication and body language. An additional benefit for group work is the preparation period, as this encourages constructive discussion of the topic and can be used to develop group skills like cooperation and negotiation.

Teaching Tips
- When developing and showing work, encourage students to look at how they can use facial expression and body language to communicate ideas as well as exploring physical levels (low, medium and high) and proximity (distance from one another)
- Fairy tales are a good place to start – give small groups different fairy tale titles and ask them to create three freeze frames (beginning, middle and end)
- A good way to explain a freeze frame is that it's like pressing the pause button on a remote control, or making a statue

Examples: *3D Living Pictures (p. 22), Bullying (p. 24), Walk on the Wild Side (p. 41)*
Related: *Action Clip, Hot Spotting, Imaginarium, Role Play, Thought Tracking*

HOT SEATING   Develop characters through questioning

- **7 years +**
- **10 minutes +**
- **Whole class, pairs and individuals**
- **Improvisation, Role Play, Speaking and Listening**

Hot Seating is a powerful way of developing a character and eliciting questions from the group. The student playing the character sits on a chair in front of the group while class members ask questions,

Start with simple facts such as name, age and occupation before moving on to more personal areas. The teacher guides the questioning in constructive directions. The student being hot-seated won't know the answer to all the questions and should be encouraged to make up imaginative responses; questions about motives and feelings are easier to answer than in-depth factual questions. It can be surprising how much detail students can come up with when they improvise answers.

Hot seating can be used with a range of students, using suitable material. It's also perfect for actors who are getting their teeth into a script. As an introduction, try *Hot Spotting*.

Teaching Tips
- Younger children can be hot-seated in pairs to give them confidence
- Don't get bogged down in facts, but concentrate on personal feelings and observations instead
- To add a touch of fun you can enlist the help of a teaching assistant or confident student to play the role of a chat show host who introduces the character and fields the questions

Examples: *If Pets Could Speak (p.14), Hit the Headlines (p. 27)*
Related: *Hot Spotting, Thought Tracking*

HOT SPOTTING   Question characters in a freeze frame

- **7 years +**
- **5 minutes**
- **Small groups**
- **Improvisation, Role Play, Speaking and Listening**

Hot Spotting is a natural progression from *Action Clip*. After watching a *Freeze Frame* come to life for a few moments, the audience may be curious about the characters and their story. Explain that this is an opportunity for them to ask questions of the characters. Encourage them to think about motivation by asking one of the characters *'Why did you do that?'* or *'How did you feel when...?'* The students in the freeze frame remain 'in the frame' but they can move and speak when questioned.

Most students will find this easier than *Hot Seating*. No-one is sitting in a chair on their own. They have the support of the group around them, plus they are actually part of a scene or story, so will feel more confident to answer. Make sure you go round the whole group so that various characters are asked questions - and that way you'll get different points of view!

The advantages of this method compared to hot seating are:
- Students are already in character
- They feel supported by other players in the freeze frame
- Questions are linked to a character's story, actions and motivations rather than 'in a void'

Example: *Bullying (p. 25), The Lost and Found Cat (p. 32)*
Related: *Action Clip, Freeze Frames, Hot Seating, Thought Tracking*

IMAGINARIUM   Explore stories and create scenes in moments

 7 years +

🕐 **10-20 minutes**

👥 **Whole class**

🌱 **Creativity, Improvisation**

It's about imagination. It's about showing how we can create a world by linking our ideas and taking a step together into the unknown. In a lot of ways, Imaginarium is the simplest drama game there is, the most unpredictable and the most flexible. It can be played just for fun or it can be used to lead into improvisation, talk, writing, art work or other spin-offs. It can be played by any age-group.

Everybody stand in a circle. I'm going to call out a theme and I want you to think of an object or person related to that theme. When you've got an idea, I want you to put up your hand. I'll pick you out and then you should step into the space and make the shape of that person, animal or object. When you make your shape, tell us who or what you are by saying 'I am a...'

Okay, the first theme is the beach. You can be anyone or anything that might be found on the beach.

So the first person puts up her hand and steps forward: *'I am a starfish.'* She makes the shape.

Stay in position because we're going to build up a picture of the beach. Who's coming next?

The next student steps forward: *'I'm a bucket.'*

Good, let's have some more. Maybe you can link to other objects on the beach or you can be on your own. And if you want, you can step in with someone else to make an object.

'I'm a spade (to go with the bucket), an ice-cream, a towel, a sun-bather, the sun, a wave, a shark, a lifeguard...'

And so the list goes on as more and more students step in, one by one. When everybody who wants to play has stepped forward, tell them:

I'm going to say a magic word and when you hear it I want you to return to your places in the circle... Whoosh!

That's how you play Imaginarium; it's fast, it's fun and it's a great way of pooling ideas or testing comprehension of a theme. It's like a physical version of brainstorming. It's a bit like *Storytelling Whoosh* (but without the storytelling).

THEMES

Hallowe'en, birthday party, Victorian inventions, Anglo-Saxons, endangered animals, global warming, four seasons, things that float, treasure chest, natural habitats (e.g. meadow, pond, tree), First World War, Jurassic Park, pirates, Nelson Mandela, food chain, ways of saving energy, objects found in the kitchen, things we saw on the school trip, haunted house, methods of transport, royal feast, picnic hamper, first aid kit

---

GENRES

Choose a genre, such as adventure, ghost, myth and legend, fantasy or science-fiction. Once the students have stepped in, question them about what they think is happening in the scene and use this as a way to spark creative writing or as a stepping-stone to acting out scenes.

We can develop the game by using tools similar to the ones we use with *Freeze Frames*.

- Tap each person on the shoulder and ask them to repeat what they are, then add an adjective: 'I'm a *wriggly* starfish, a *rusty* bucket, a *melting* ice-cream'
- Tap people on the shoulder and ask them to speak their thoughts aloud (*Thought Tracking*)
- Bring the scene to life with *Action Clip*
- Create a *Soundscape* using the characters and objects

Teaching Tips

- It's important that players watch and listen carefully so that they add in an appropriate character or object
- Only one idea at a time should be added so that everyone can see and hear what's being included
- With a larger class, it often works best to go round the circle in order. Not everybody has to step in (those who didn't have a go can play next time)
- Players should think about how their characters and objects relate to each other, how they can make interesting shapes and how they can use different levels (high, medium or low)
- If you're rehearsing a play, use the game as a brainstorming activity to create inspiring ideas for the director and actors
- Take photos of the finished scene for future reference

Examples: *Funnybones (p. 10), Hit The Headlines (p. 26), Science and Drama (p. 36)*
Related: *Action Clip, Freeze Frames, Improvisation, Storytelling Whoosh, Thought Tracking*

LOCATIONS

Amusement park, archaeological museum, Buckingham Palace, bus stop, circus, city street, classroom, farmyard, garden shed, gym, mad scientist's laboratory, map of Europe, moon base, outer space, rainforest, restaurant, shopping mall, toy box, treasure island, Tutankhamun's tomb, under the sea

---

STORIES AND PLAYS

Choose a particular location or moment in a story, a specific scene or chapter - or just explore the whole story with characters and objects.

Anansi's jungle, Camelot, Cinderella's house, Cittàgazze, Farmer Duck's farmyard, Funnybones' park, Gingerbread house, Gruffalo forest, Harry Potter's bedroom, Hobbit-hole, Hogwarts' dining room, King Midas' palace, Juliet's garden on a moonlit night, Labyrinth of the Minotaur, Macbeth's castle, Matilda's classroom, Mr Wonka's chocolate factory, Narnia, Pandora's box, Prospero's Island, Robin Hood's forest, Sherlock Holmes' parlour, Stig's dump, Toad Hall, Tom's midnight garden

IMPROVISATION — Spontaneous performance of a scene or story

Improvisation is familiar to children as a natural element of play, enabling them to imaginatively explore any situation and its potential outcomes. In educational drama, improvisation develops pupils' confidence, encouraging them to be creative, to cooperate, negotiate, speak and listen to each other. It can be done at any time and requires no lines to be learned. This collective story-making enables students to quickly share ideas and views with each other and is an effective way of motivating children to write. Improvisation is an effective way of communicating ideas or exploring a story or theme.

Improvisation can be done individually, in pairs, groups or as a whole class. It usually involves speech and movement but can be silent. Although it is created spontaneously, improvisation needs structure, ranging from an opening line to a defined theme or specific situation. Partner work is a great place to start, for example, a conversation on a theme or an activity enacted together.

Teaching Tips

- To establish an improvised situation, try asking the questions 'Who?', 'What?', 'Where?', 'When?' and 'Why?'
- Remind children about stories having a beginning, middle and end – and give them a time limit.
- A good way to develop improvisation is to start with a freeze-frame, then use *Thought Tracking* and *Action Clip*

Examples: *Pair Improvisation (p. 18), Skype Call (p. 34), Animal Habitats (p. 40)*
Related: *Action Clip, Freeze Frames, Hot Spotting, Role Play, Thought Tracking*

ROLE PLAY — Explore viewpoints of other characters

For most children, the ability to step into another character's shoes through make-believe play comes naturally. By adopting a role, students can explore contrasting viewpoints, step into the past or future and travel to different locations, dealing with issues on emotional, moral and intellectual levels. They grapple with problems, deal with success and failure in the knowledge that it is only make-believe.

Role play enables students to be objective about imagined learning so that they can talk about what happened whilst they were 'pretending to be someone else' and learn from their experiences. They need to comprehend what happens during the shared fiction so that they can understand implications for their own behaviour in the real world.

More ideas about using role play can be found in Farmer, D. (2011). *Learning Through Drama in the Primary Years*. CreateSpace. ISBN 978-1466445253

Examples: *Shopping Role Play (p. 18), Guess Who I Am (p. 23), Bullying (p. 24)*
Related: *Hot Seating, Improvisation, Teacher in Role*

SOUNDSCAPES
Creating atmospheres through sound

- **7 years +**
- **10 minutes +**
- **Whole class**
- **Improvisation, Speaking and Listening**

Soundscapes enable students to create an evocative 'sound picture' of a scene or mood, which can be used to help them imagine the location of a story or create a soundtrack for performance.

Select a theme such as a beach, city or jungle. Sit the pupils in a group and ask them for examples of sounds that might be heard in this environment. Explain that the group is going to 'paint a picture' using sounds – using their voices (and body percussion if appropriate). Designate sections of the group to make different sounds so that you have a 'human orchestra'.

The teacher conducts the overall shape of the soundscape by raising her hand to increase the volume or bringing it to touch her lap for silence. Sections of the group can be faded in and out as appropriate so that all the sounds are heard. After you have tried it out, ask for feedback then try again to improve the result.

It can be helpful to provide a structure for the soundscape, such as 'a day in the rainforest', 'a storm at sea', or 'a walk through the marketplace' so that sounds evolve during the piece. You may choose to use simple percussion instruments or everyday objects that make suitable sounds. This works better if you give children an opportunity to explore the sounds they can make with the instruments and to identify which are most appropriate for the soundscape in advance.

Examples: *The Tiger Child (p. 4), Funnybones (p. 10), 3D Living Pictures (p. 23), A Midsummer Night's Dream (p. 48)*
Related: *Imaginarium, Storytelling Whoosh*

GET INTO THE GROOVE

Playing recorded music can add a whole new dimension to drama activities. Not only does it provide atmosphere and emotion, but it has been shown to have many other benefits such as improving memory and reducing anxiety. In addition it really inspires students if the drama activity involves a lot of movement.

Try different styles of music, from classical to modern and contemporary, orchestral to jazz, pop and punk (depending on the atmosphere you are trying to create!)

SPEAKING OBJECTS

Create characters from objects

- 👫 5 years +
- 🕐 10 minutes +
- 👥 Whole class, Small groups, Pairs
- 🎭 Improvisation, Speaking and Listening

Just as students can take on the role of a character, so they can also represent the viewpoint of an object. Speaking as an object enables students to gain a deeper understanding of a situation by seeing it from an unusual viewpoint. Think of it as a combination of *Freeze Frames* and *Thought Tracking*.

If working in pairs or small groups, students can be related objects – such as a pair of shoes or a box of toys. When working as a larger group or whole class, pupils can become speaking objects in a particular place such as furniture in a living room or items in a shop window. Once the theme has been set, students are invited to step into the space and make a shape one at a time, stating the object they represent. Some students can remain outside the space in order to ask questions of the objects.

Examples

- Objects in a first-aid kit explain how they help in an emergency
- Artefacts found in an archaeological dig describe what they might have been used for
- Items in a second-hand shop talk about where they used to live and who used to own them

Example: *Packing the Rucksack (p. 35)*
Related: *Imaginarium, Ten Second Objects, Thought Tracking*

SPOTLIGHT

Focus on groups/parts of scenes

- 👫 5 years +
- 🕐 5 minutes
- 👥 Whole class, Small groups
- 🎭 Improvisation, Speaking and Listening

Imagine that your hand is a spotlight. If you have a number of groups sitting ready to show their work, walk around the space then shine your 'spotlight' over a group to indicate that the members should come to life. You can also use it when a large group (or the whole class) are making a *Freeze Frame*. In this case, use spotlight to focus on different parts of the scene. Walk through the group and hold your hand above parts of the scene to indicate which characters should come to life and be heard. Choose pairs of students, smaller sub-groups or individuals as appropriate.

Example: *3D Living Pictures (p. 23)*
Related: *Best Bits, Freeze Frames*

STOP, GO, JUMP, CLAP   Movement and character warm-up game

 5 years +

10 minutes

Whole class

Concentration, Movement, Warm Up

PART ONE

Ask the class to spread out in the space. Explain that the students need to learn four simple actions. Begin with 'Stop' and 'Go', encouraging students to listen and respond quickly. 'Go' means walk around the space and 'Stop' means stop as still as a statue. Once students are confident with these instructions, introduce 'Jump' (jump in the air) and 'Clap' (everyone should clap at the same time). After a while combine these instructions in a random order, for example, 'go, stop, jump, clap, go, clap'.

PART TWO

When they have got the hang of Part One, introduce the next challenge:

Now we're entering an alternate universe. In this universe, 'Stop' means 'Go', 'Go' means 'Stop' — and of course 'Clap' means 'Jump' and 'Jump' means 'Clap'!

As you try out these new commands on the class, go easy as it will take students a while to get used to the new meanings. However, it usually causes much hilarity and head-scratching.

PART THREE

This optional part is perfect for exploring characters, emotions and activities. Explain that we are returning to the normal universe, so all the commands will regain their original meanings: 'Go' means 'Go', 'Stop' means 'Stop' and so on.

Now explain that the next time you call 'Stop' you will also say 'Show Me...' and then the name of a character. They should make a statue of that character.

Make your very best statue of the character. When I say 'Go' can you move as that character would move? Can you 'Jump' as the character would jump and 'Clap' as they would clap?

After a while, stop them again and introduce the next character. You can also use an emotion or activity.

Optional: Once they have made a few characters, can they slowly transform from one character to another on the count of five?

Characters, Emotions and Activities
– Dracula, Winnie the Pooh, Sherlock Holmes, Cruella DeVille, Cheshire Cat, Puck, Juliet, Peter Pan
– Astronaut, dog trainer, fire-fighter, hairdresser, plumber, spy, nurse, pop star, supermarket assistant
– Amazed, depressed, angry, nervous, proud, in love, confused, shocked, terrified, jealous, excited
– Driving, golfing, knitting, playing piano, skiing, washing dishes, writing, eating chips, teaching

Example: *A Midsummer Night's Dream (p. 49)*
Related: *Ten Second Objects*

STORYTELLING WHOOSH! | Act out a story as it is told

- **5 years +**
- **10-20 minutes**
- **Whole class**
- **Improvisation, Role Play**
- **Prepared Story**

Storytelling Whoosh[1] is an engaging and interactive way of involving the whole class to instantly bring a story to life. It requires no rehearsal and can be used with any age-group from pre-school to adult. It taps into the innate propensity we all have for acting out stories as we tell them. The teacher's role is that of a storyteller, while the students play characters, objects, places or events in the story, whether it be Hermione Grainger, a throne, a pumpkin or a stormy sea.

Gather the class into a circle (sitting or standing). I usually explain it like this:

I'm going to tell you a story and everybody here will have the chance to act it out. You'll have the chance to play people and even objects. As I tell the story I'll go round the circle and point to people. So if I point to you, I want you to get up, move into the circle and make the shape of an object or become a character. You may have to move around or even speak - but don't worry, I'll tell you what to say.

Once upon a time, in a far off land there was...

Start telling the story and as soon as a character or object is mentioned, signal to the student next to you to step into the circle to become the character or make a freeze frame. If more than one character is mentioned then a few players can step in together (this is handy for larger groups). An object can be made by several people – for example, a forest or ship.

Continue with the story, going round the circle of students in order. That way, the assignment of characters is made randomly and regardless of gender. It's not only democratic but often amusing! When you finish a section of the story, or if the space inside the circle is busy, just say:

Now I'm going to wave my arms and say a magic word. And when I do, everybody in the circle will return to their places.

Now wave your arms dramatically and say *'Whoosh!'*

When everyone has returned to their places, continue the narrative and select the next person whose turn it is to play a character. That way, everybody gets a chance to participate and the same character will be played by several different people. Students could be a toadstool one time and a wizard the next.

If appropriate, the whole group can take part at once – for example, as a castle, crowd or storm. During the story, characters can interact with one another and speak improvised dialogue or repeat lines spoken by you. You can say 'Whoosh!' as many times as necessary during the story – it's a powerful secret weapon! Participants will listen to, take part in and most of all remember the story because they helped to create and tell it.

Examples: *The Tiger Child (p. 6), A Midsummer Night's Dream (pp. 50-51)*
Related: *Freeze Frames, Imaginarium, Improvisation, Role Play*

---

[1]   'Storytelling Whoosh' was devised by Professor Joe Winston of The University of Warwick and subsequently developed for use as part of The Royal Shakespeare Company's education programme.

TEACHER IN ROLE   Guide the action through role play

 5 years +

 10 minutes +

Whole class

Improvisation, Role Play

Teacher in Role enables the teacher (or other adult) to directly participate in the dramatic process and influence it from the *inside*. It's an instant way of setting a scene and directly involving students. Children are used to stepping into and out of role in everyday play and are likely to be keen to participate.

The approach does not require great acting skills. It can be seen as an extension of the ever-changing role-play that we all initiate – whether as parent, child, teacher, student, colleague and so on. The strategy simply involves 'stepping into somebody else's shoes' for a while to put forward their point of view. This can be done by subtly changing your tone of voice and body language to communicate key attitudes, emotions and viewpoints. If you can use different voices for characters when you tell a story then you are certainly able to carry out teacher in role.

The use of a token prop or piece of costume helps to clarify when you are stepping in and out of role: *'When I put on this scarf I will be Paddington Bear'* or *'When I sit in this chair I will be the Minotaur'*. If you are unsure how to begin, try *Hot-Seating* first. This will give you valuable experience of assuming a role in relation to the students and responding to their comments and questions. Hot-seating becomes teacher in role when you start to take the lead in the discussion or when you encourage pupils to deepen their involvement. This can be as simple as walking around and engaging with individual students or involving them in occupational mime activities to deepen their belief.

Status

You may choose to play a high-status character, an equal, or subordinate role – whatever is useful in developing the drama.

High status

An authoritative role such as an official or other commanding character enables you to remain in control and give clear guidance. While this is an attractive option, it can be perceived as similar to your usual teaching role and thus inhibit students in their willingness to become involved.

Equal status

An equal role enables you to be 'one of them' – a fellow villager, jury member, explorer and so on. You are in the same predicament as the children but can guide by asking questions.

Low status

You can still maintain the focus of the class by playing a low-status role – someone in need of help or guidance. Students are likely to be sympathetic to such a character as it puts them in an 'expert' role.

- For further guidance and examples, see Farmer, D. (2011). *Learning Through Drama in the Primary Years*. CreateSpace. ISBN 978-1466445253

Examples: *The Tiger Child (p. 6), The King's Sentence (p. 18), The Lost and Found Cat (pp. 32-33)*
Related: *Hot Seating, Role Play*

TEN SECOND OBJECTS — Group objects created in a flash

ŤŤ 7 years +

🕐 10 seconds

⚑ Small groups (4-6)

👤 Improvisation, Movement, Warm Up

This is one of my favourite games. I use it in just about every workshop I run. It doesn't require any materials, just imagination!

This game is called Ten Second Objects. In this game your group is going to make the shape of an object, using everybody in the group, joining together in some way. I'm going to call out the name of an object and then you've got ten seconds to make the object out of yourselves.

As everyone looks at each other, the light dawns on them - they're going to have to work fast. They smile or laugh - nervously. But don't give them time to think about it.

The first object is a... car. Off you go, ten, nine, eight, seven, six...

By now the groups are working quickly, a few words are spoken as students move into place.

Remember, everyone has to join in, even if you are a windscreen wiper! Find a place in your group. Five, four, three, two, one... and freeze! Well done, everybody. Brilliant. Each group has made the shape of a car and they are all different. Let's have a look at them.

The students can sit down and watch as each group shows what they've made. I assure them that there is no right or wrong answer in this game. It's all about working together. Now that the groups have realised how easy it is, I move straight on to the next object.

Teaching Tips

– Quite often children will have moving parts in their object - and sounds (for example, crackling flames in a fire). I'll ask them to freeze at the end of ten seconds so that order is restored. Then when groups show their object I ask them to bring it to life for a few moments (or if it's a machine, I mime pressing the 'on' button)

– You may want to start your session by demonstrating how the game works with one group of volunteers while everybody else watches. Usually this is very funny and makes other people want to have a go

– Objects can be big (the Statue of Liberty) or small (a pencil-sharpener). When groups have made a few you can ask them to make up one of their own for others to guess. Give them a whole thirty seconds for this! And towards the end start counting down the last ten seconds

– The whole beauty of *Ten Second Objects* is that it only takes... 10 seconds. This means that players don't have time to argue, they just have to get on. The time-limit gives them a challenge and when they see other groups working on their ideas it usually acts as a kind of peer-pressure (in a positive way) to speed them up

Examples: *Tiger Child (p. 4), Funnybones (pp. 8-10), Hit The Headlines (p. 26)*

Related: *Freeze Frames, Imaginarium, Speaking Objects*

FAVOURITES ♥

Bus/Car, Clock, Fire, Firework/
Volcano, Flower, Giraffe (or other
animal), Helicopter, Musical
instrument, Pirate ship, Plate
of food for breakfast, Toaster,
Washing machine

SCIENCE/STEM

2D/3D shapes, Bar graph, Beehive,
Bridge, Chemical reaction, Compass,
Constellations, Digestive system,
Molecule, Electrical circuit, Light bulb,
Snowflake, Steam engine, Storm
cloud, Wind farm

HISTORY ⛰

Boudicca's chariot, Mayan pyramid,
Moai, Norman castle, Sphinx, Sutton Hoo
helmet, Titanic, Tutankhamun's tomb,
Tyrannosaurus Rex, Victorian inventions,
Viking longboat, Wooden Horse of Troy,
WW2 gas mask

FAMOUS PLACES 🏰

Buckingham Palace, Disneyland, Eiffel Tower,
Grand Canyon, Great Barrier Reef, Great Wall
of China, Iguazú Falls, International Space
Station, Leaning Tower of Pisa, London Eye,
London Tower Bridge, Statue of Liberty,
Sydney Opera House, Taj Mahal

RANDOM OBJECTS 🎲

Bike, Birthday cake, Bouncy castle, Butterfly, Car wash, Carousel, Dishwasher, Dragon, Drone,
Emotions, Escalator, Fire engine/truck with ladder, Hamster on a wheel, Hot air balloon,
Hot dog, Jack in a box, Jigsaw puzzle, Jukebox, Letters and numbers, Mosque, Motorway,
Paddle Steamer, Pencil sharpener, Photocopier, Picasso painting, Pinball machine, Pizza,
Playground equipment, Rainbow, Rainforest, Scissors, Sewing machine, Snow globe,
Snowman, Stapler, Teacher's desk drawer, Time machine, Transport, Treasure Chest, UFO,
Unicorn, Vending machine, Wax Museum

AMUSEMENT PARK 🎡

Bumper cars, Candy-floss,
Fairy-tale castle, Ferris wheel,
Fireworks, Ghost train, Log
flume, Merry-go-round, Popcorn
Machine, Roller coaster, Turnstile

HALLOWE'EN 🎃

Bat, Broomstick, Cauldron,
Cobweb, Ghost, Haunted house,
Mummy, Pumpkin, Skeleton,
Spider, Tombstone, Treat, Trick,
Vampire, Witch, Zombie

THOUGHT TRACKING

Speak a character's thoughts aloud

- **5 years +**
- **5 minutes**
- **Small groups**
- **Improvisation**

Thought Tracking is used in conjunction with *Freeze Frames*. When participants are frozen in position, explain that you will tap them on the shoulder – and when you do, you would like them to speak aloud the thoughts or feelings of their character. This is usually in the first-person i.e. 'I am feeling worried' rather than 'She is worried.'

Thought tracking is an effective way of progressing from freeze frames to speech and then on to extended improvisation. Simply holding a pose enables participants to empathise more closely with the role and most children will find it easy to express their character's thoughts. Less confident or younger participants may just say a word or two but will soon gain confidence to express themselves in longer sentences. It doesn't take long to thought-track each member of a group so that you can reveal a wide range of attitudes and feelings from different characters.

Teaching Tips

Encourage younger students with prompts such as:
- I can see, hear, feel, smell, taste...
- I wish...
- I wonder...
- I hope...
- I feel...
- I imagine...

If a child is nervous or unsure what to say, just ask other students for suggestions – usually there will be no shortage of ideas.

Even if students are playing an inanimate object or animal in a freeze frame, they can still speak their thoughts aloud. If they choose to make a sound instead of words, encourage them by saying something like 'if the helicopter/seagull could talk, what would it say?'

Examples: *If Pets Could Speak (p. 14), 3D Living Pictures (p. 26), The Lost and Found Cat (pp. 31-32)*
Related: *Action Clip, Freeze Frames*

WHERE DO YOU STAND?   Express your opinion

7 years +

10-15 minutes

Whole class

Decision Making, Speaking and Listening

Stand two chairs a long way apart and put a sign on them saying 'Agree' and 'Disagree' or 'Thumbs up/ Thumbs down' signs (pp. 70-71). Read out a statement and ask everybody to choose a place to stand in between the chairs that they feel represents their view. The nearer they stand to one of the chairs, the stronger the opinion they are expressing. Those who are not sure, are open-minded or don't want to say can move towards the middle. Emphasise that everybody's point of view will be respected and encourage each person to decide for themselves. Give them a few moments to make their decision.

Once they have chosen their spot you can ask individuals why they decided to stand where they are. Gather a few opinions from different students in the space. Finally you can ask if anyone would like to change position now that they've heard differing points of view. This helps students to take other people's views into consideration.

Suggested Topics

I prefer cats to dogs
Pizza is better than fish and chips
I prefer playing computer games to sports
I'd rather stroke a snake than hold a spider
I'd rather be Shere Khan than Baloo
If you find money on the street you should be allowed to keep it
Precious jewels are more valuable than trees
It's OK to borrow something from a friend without asking them
It's better to get angry than to bottle it up
Old people just don't understand young people (or vice-versa)

Teaching Tips

- Like *Conscience Alley*, this game can be used to explore a decision faced by a character as well as moral dilemmas. For example, everyone chooses (or is given) a character from a story. Suitable statements could be *'My character makes great decisions'* or *'My character likes helping people'*
- The activity is ideal for practising the use of persuasive language

Examples: *If Pets Could Speak (p. 15), Bullying (p. 25), Global Warming: Problems and Solutions (p. 39)*
Related: *Conscience Alley*

THUMBS UP (Where Do You Stand? p.69)

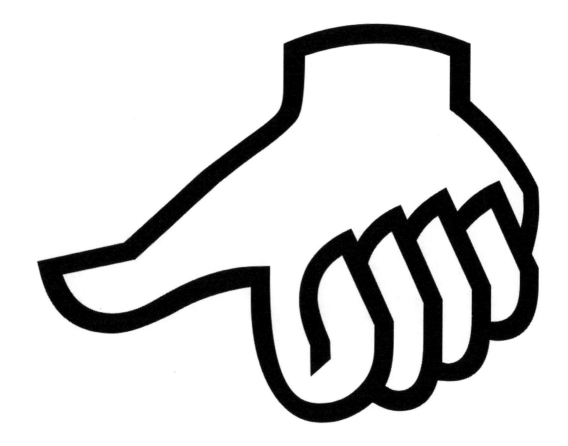

THUMBS UP (Where Do You Stand? p.69)

THUMBS UP (Where Do You Stand? p.69)

© Drama Resource 2021 | Where Do You Stand?

© Drama Resource 2021 | The Magic Box (pp. 2-3) | Illustration by John Shelley

© Drama Resource 2021 | The Tiger Child (pp.4-7) | Illustration by John Shelley

© Drama Resource 2021 | Funnybones (pp. 8-11) | Illustration by John Shelley

© Drama Resource 2021 | Bullying (pp. 24-25) | Illustration by John Shelley

© Drama Resource 2021 | The Lost and Found Cat (pp. 30-34) | Illustration by John Shelley

© Drama Resource 2021 | A Midsummer Night's Dream (pp. 48-51) | Illustration by John Shelley

MAKE YOUR OWN CARDS

FURTHER READING | Other books by David Farmer

101 DRAMA GAMES AND ACTIVITIES

This best-selling book (over 20,000 copies) was developed during a wide-ranging career in education and theatre, through workshops with actors, teachers and children around the world. The pages are packed with tried and tested ideas for a whole range of activities useful for drama lessons, workshops or rehearsals. Sections include improvisation, mime, ice-breakers, group dynamics, rehearsal, story-telling, voice and warm-ups.

"David Farmer's excellent book ...it is here that you will more than likely find an activity that will suit your needs."

- Journal of National Drama

101 MORE DRAMA GAMES AND ACTIVITIES

This sequel to the classic '101 Drama Games and Activities' contains inspirational games and exercises to use in drama lessons and workshops as well as during rehearsal and devising periods. There are activities to develop concentration, mime, movement and team building plus dozens of ideas for developing improvisation and exploring storytelling skills.

"...bubbles over with imaginative ideas which could be used to good effect by non-specialist as well as seasoned drama teachers. Excellent resource for primary, secondary and other drama teachers."

- Teaching Drama Magazine.

LEARNING THROUGH DRAMA IN THE PRIMARY YEARS

The book provides guidance to teachers who have never taught drama before but are considering using it in a subject area such as science or history and offers new approaches to those familiar with common drama techniques. The book includes 36 drama strategies and over 250 cross-curricular activities, including practical ideas for inspiring speaking, listening and writing.

'Even the well-practiced and creative drama teacher will find something in this book that serves as a refresher, reminder or quite simply a new idea... a must-have publication for those serious about the teaching of drama in primary school settings.'

- Teaching Drama magazine.

PLAYFUL PLAYS: VOLUME ONE

This lively collection of eight short plays for children and young people is supported by inspirational drama games designed to bring creativity and fun to the rehearsal room. The stories are based on traditional folk-tales from countries including China, Ghana, Greece, Japan, Turkey and Scandinavia. The plays feature performance techniques such as mime, mask, freeze frames, audience participation, live music and song.

"It offers teachers an off-the-shelf, ready-to-go, high-quality rehearsal process ideal for primary-aged students... The book is very well laid out and user-friendly, and is the perfect go-to for short presentation pieces that pack a punch."

- Teaching Drama Magazine.

Printed in Great Britain
by Amazon

23749082R10048